P9-AFJ-227

MACHO
MACHO
Animals

Other *Pearls Before Swine* Collections

The Sopratos
Da Brudderhood of Zeeba Zeeba Eata
The Ratvolution Will Not Be Televised
Nighthogs
This Little Piggy Stayed Home
BLTs Taste So Darn Good

Treasuries

The Crass Menagerie
Lions and Tigers and Crocs, Oh My!
Sgt. Piggy's Lonely Hearts Club Comic

Gift Book

Da Crockydile Book o' Frendsheep

A PEARLS BEFORE SWINE Collection by Stephan Pastis

Andrews McMeel
Publishing, LLC

Kansas City

Pearls Before Swine is distributed internationally by United Feature Syndicate.

 For information, write Andrews McMeel Publishing, LLC, an Andrews McMeel Universal company, 1130 Walnut Street, Kansas City, Missouri 64106.

08 09 10 11 12 BBG 10 9 8 7 6 5 4 3 2 1

ISBN-13: 978-0-7407-7369-3
ISBN-10: 0-7407-7369-0

Library of Congress Control Number: 2008922539

www.andrewsmcmeel.com

Pearls Before Swine can be viewed on the Internet at
www.comics.com/comics/pearls.

These strips appeared in newspapers from August 7, 2006, to May 13, 2007.

For Tom and Julia, who occupy the center of my heart

Foreword

by Bil Keane, creator of *The Family Circus*

Thank you for sending me a rough copy of *Macho Macho Animals*. I will waste no time reading it and will not have my good name defiled by writing a foreword for a book written by a reprobate. This unprincipled character has the audacity to think that I will do a foreword for a book he is writing—no way! This moron expects me to write a foreword and besmirch my good name.

Look, I have a reputation to uphold. I'd be a hypocrite if I wrote a foreword for his book. Before he became a cartoonist, Pastis was an attorney. He is a perfect example of making himself a worm. He now works at the Charles M. Schulz Museum in Santa Rosa, California. He's their prime exhibit of how not to be a cartoonist. His father lives in Arizona, not too far from my home, and he never admits to anyone that his son draws *Pearls Before Swine*. Stephan comes to see his poor old dad once every decade! That's the kind of hypocrite he is. No way will I do a foreword for his book. He's a jack-of-all-trades, but a master of none.

I'm being asked to do a foreword for the most mean-spirited person I know. There is no way that I would even consider this request from a guy that has insulted me, insulted my family, and insulted the *Family Circus*. He is the one who drew a cartoon showing his character Rat (and that is him; he is the reprobate) interacting with the *Family Circus* characters. He once drew a cartoon showing my *Family Circus* characters as the butt of his mean-spirited humor. He had the audacity to draw Osama Bin Laden, turban and all, sitting with Mommy, Jeffy, and Dolly at dinner in their home. Mommy is saying, "I'm sorry, Osama, but at the end of grace, we say 'Amen,' not 'Death to America.'"

That is the kind of material I have been putting up with, and now he has the gall to ask me to do the favor of writing a foreword! I can go on and on about all the insults I have endured.

He did a Sunday page showing Jeffy following a dotted line through the neighborhood bar, a gang initiation, and a casino; stealing a car; robbing a liquor store; getting tattooed; and entering a restaurant. The final panel shows Pig, Rat (Pastis), and Jeffy. Jeffy says, "So I'm battling a few demons."

He is the guy battling demons. I have no intention of writing a foreword for his book as that is doing him a favor and he certainly does not deserve it!

RAT... IT'S ME, GARY, YOUR MANAGER AT THE COFFEE SHOP... WHY AREN'T YOU HERE?
BECAUSE CAPITALISM IS A CRUEL OPPRESSOR OF THE SOUL... JOIN ME, GARY... LET US THROW OURSELVES UPON THE GEARS OF THE MACHINERY.
Joe's

GET YOUR @## IN HERE.
OH, RELAX, YOU TALKING SUIT... I GOT SOMEONE TO COVER FOR ME... HE SHOULD BE THERE BY NOW... LOOK FOR HIM... HE'S GREEN.
GREEN?

Customer bad. May me bite off head?
OH LORD.
Joe's ROASTERY

A CROCODILE?? YOU SENT A CROCODILE TO REPLACE YOU AT THIS CAFE??
TAKE IT EASY. THAT CROC IS TOTALLY QUALIFIED.
Joe's ROASTERY

QUALIFIED? HE EATS MAMMALS! MY CUSTOMERS ARE MAMMALS!! THAT IS NOT AN OPTIMAL ARRANGEMENT!!
LISTEN, HOMEY... THAT CROC IS AN INCOMPETENT PREDATOR. NOW UNLESS YOUR CUSTOMER IS A SELF-ABSORBED BOOKWORM, THERE'S NO WAY HE WON'T SEE HIM COMING.
THIS... IS... A... CAFE
Joe's ROASTER

OH, WE ARE SO NOT COMING BACK HERE.

Let me get straight... You fire me?
OF COURSE I'M FIRING YOU!!
Joe's ROASTERY

But me was on time.
YOU... KILLED... A... CUSTOMER.
Joe's ROASTERY

...Nobody perfect, Bob.
Joe's ROASTERY

"God grant me da serenity to accept da prey me no can catch.
Courage to catch da prey me can.
And da wisdom teef to chew da big ones."

WHAT ARE YOU READING?
IT'S A LETTER FROM THE NATIONAL CARTOONISTS SOCIETY...LOOKS LIKE THEY'RE CHANGING SOME OF THE RULES FOR THE COMICS.
8/13

WHAT'D THEY CHANGE?
WELL, IT SAYS HERE THAT RIGHT NOW, THE ONLY TWO COMIC STRIPS THAT ARE ACTUALLY HAVING THEIR CHARACTERS AGE ARE "BABY BLUES" AND "FOR BETTER OR FOR WORSE."

SO?
WELL, ACCORDING TO THEM, IT'S NOT FAIR THAT CERTAIN CHARACTERS HAVE TO AGE WHILE OTHERS GET TO REMAIN FROZEN IN TIME.

SO WHAT ARE THEY GONNA DO?
ACCORDING TO THIS, "IT SHALL BE THE RESPONSIBILITY OF ALL CURRENT SYNDICATED CARTOONISTS TO ADVANCE THEIR CHARACTERS TO THE AGE THEY WOULD PRESENTLY BE, BASED UPON THE START DATE OF THE COMIC."

WELL, THAT SHOULDN'T BE TOO BAD FOR A STRIP LIKE OURS... WE'RE ONLY FOUR YEARS OLD.

YEAH, RUB IT IN, YOU BIG, FAT @&!%@&@ PIG.
WHAT'S IT TAKE FOR JEFFY TO GET A @#&@ MARTINI AROUND HERE?!
CALL THE BOUNCER.
AGAIN?

"Faster, Mommy, faster!"

"Get a job, Billy."

"And remember...No telling Mommy I shot my probation officer."

THIS RULE REQUIRING ALL COMICS TO MAKE THEIR CHARACTERS THE AGE THEY SHOULD REALLY BE HAS GOT TO GO.
IT ENDS TOMORROW. THEY JUST ANNOUNCED IT.

OH, GOOD... BECAUSE READING MY FAVORITE STRIP, "BLONDIE," JUST WASN'T THE SAME.
8/17

DON'T TELL ME YOU'RE GONNA EAT THAT WHOLE SANDWICH!
BUMSTEAD R.I.P.
BUMSTEAD R.I.P.

WHAT ARE YOU DOING?
RESEARCHING TRIPS TO THE SOUTH POLE... I'M THINKING ABOUT VISITING MY PAL, OLLIE THE PENGUIN. HE'S THE ONE WITH THE OVERPROTECTIVE MOM.

BUT ALL THOSE STUPID PENGUINS LOOK ALIKE... HOW WOULD YOU EVEN FIND HIM?
8/18

8/19

I'M NOT GOING IN LIKE THIS, MOM.
HUSH, SWEETIE.

Rat's Travel Guide to the World's Great Cities
Chapter 2: Calcutta
PROS
Warm. Cheap.
Not too touristy.
CONS
Burgers: Hard to find.
Cockiest. Cows. Ever.
8/20

THE CROCS ARE GOING TO COLLEGE.
WHAT FOR?

TO GET SMARTER.
COLLEGE LECTURES DO NOT MAKE YOU SMARTER.
8/21

THEN WHAT'S THEIR EFFECT?

zzzZzzZz

THE CROCS ATTEND COLLEGE
...AND THAT, SIR, IS WHAT I BELIEVE ENGELS MEANT BY EGALITARIANISM.
VERY PROVOCATIVE, MR. TRIPODES...I SEE YOU'VE STUDIED HARD.

WHY DON'T WE GET SOMEONE ELSE INVOLVED HERE?.. HOW 'BOUT YOU, SIR? WHAT DO YOU THINK ENGELS MEANT BY EGALITARIANISM?

8/22

What time recess?

SIR... THE SMITTYS PARKED THEIR CAR IN FRONT OF OUR HOUSE AGAIN.
IS THAT BAD?

YESSIR... IN A NEIGHBORHOOD WHERE EVERYONE HAS THEIR OWN GARAGES, IT'S GENERALLY CONSIDERED RUDE TO CONTINUALLY PARK YOUR CAR IN FRONT OF YOUR NEIGHBOR'S HOUSE.

THEN LEAVE A LITTLE REMINDER ON THEIR WINDSHIELD.

8/23
DEFINE 'REMINDER.'

SIR, GOOD MORNING, SIR... AT APPROXIMATELY 2300 LAST NIGHT, ONE OF THE FOGGINI KIDS THREW A PROJECTILE AT OUR BASE.
WHAT DID THEY THROW??

THIS, SIR... FORTUNATELY, IT LANDED ON SOFT GRASS AND DID NOT BREAK.
BUT IT'S JUST AN EGG.
8/24

SIR, I'M A DUCK, SIR.. THIS COULD BE KIN! YOU DON'T SEE ME THROWING PREGNANT ITALIAN WOMEN AT THEIR PORCH, DO YOU?!?!

WHOA WHOA WHOA... TAKE IT EEEEEASY, LI'L GUARD DUCK.
THANK YOU, SIR.. BUT I CAN DO WITHOUT THE MAN HUG.

Dear Croc Brudders,
Too morrow me have test.

Me no study. Me no reed. Me no stay wake in class. But me got Plan "B".
8/25

Hope teecher hit by Bus.

THE CROCS ATTEND COLLEGE
"...AND SO, IN CONCLUSION, THE GREEN LIGHT ON DAISY'S DOCK SYMBOLIZED A DREAM UNFULFILLED, A TANGIBLE REMINDER OF THE IMPLAUSIBILITY OF GATSBY'S ASPIRATION."
A SUPERB ESSAY, MR. FOGLIANI.

AND WHY DON'T WE GO NEXT TO THE YOUNG FELLOW NEXT TO YOU... SIR, LET'S HEAR YOUR ESSAY ON GATSBY'S CONCLUSION, AS WELL AS ITS SIGNIFICANCE AND HOW IT ALL TIES IN TO FITZGERALD'S USE OF COLOR SYMBOLISM.

8/26

"Green is my favoritest color."

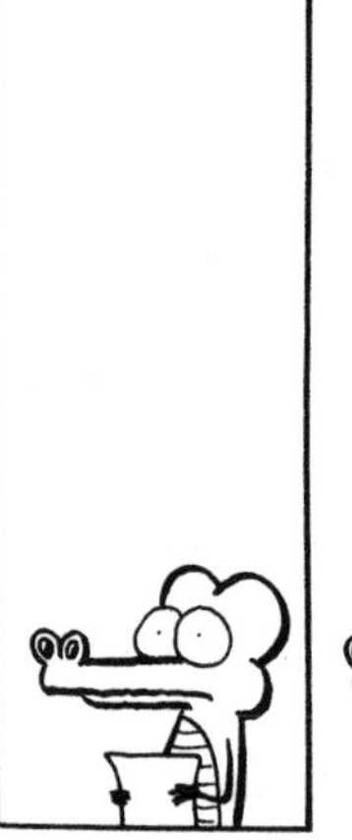

Peese drive home safely.

HEY, RAT.. I'D LIKE YOU TO MEET MY FRIEND, TOM RICHMOND... HE'S PROBABLY THE BEST CARICATURIST IN THE COUNTRY.
PLEASE, DUDE. ALL THOSE GUYS DO IS EXAGGERATE SOMEBODY'S FEATURES. I CAN DO THAT.

OH, YEAH?.. HERE.. WHY DON'T YOU BOTH DRAW, SAY, UH.. BARBRA STREISAND, AND WE'LL SEE WHOSE WORK IS BETTER.
FINE... PREPARE TO LOSE, MUSCLEHEAD.

DRAW DRAW DRAW DRAW
DRAW DRAW DRAW
...TIME'S UP. LET'S SEE YOURS, TOM.

WOW.
AMAZING.
TERRIFIC! LET'S SEE YOURS NOW, RAT.....

8/27

LOOKS LIKE A TIE.

SOCIOLOGY 101:
Midterm Essay Exam
Identify the root causes of poverty.

Lack of moneys.

Dat was easy.

Dear Pigita, ♥ I Love You. You Are Smart. You are beautiful. I am so lucky to Have You for A girlfriend.

YOU STUPID PIG. GIRLS DON'T LIKE NICE GUYS. THEY GO FOR THE BAD BOYS, THE REBELS... GUYS WHO ARE RECKLESS AND UNCARING...

P.S. Today I left the twisty off the Wonder Bread.

SIR, BAD NEWS, SIR...THE POLLS ARE IN AND 74 PERCENT OF THE NEIGHBORHOOD DISAPPROVES OF ME.

THAT DOESN'T SURPRISE ME, LI'L GUARD DUCK. YOU KNOW WHAT YOU'RE GONNA HAVE TO DO, DON'T YOU?

THREATEN AND INTIMIDATE 74 PERCENT OF THE NEIGHBORHOOD?

I'VE GUESSED WRONG, HAVEN'T I, SIR?

WHAT DO YOU GOT THERE?
THREE PACKAGES OF BACON.

WHO CARES ABOUT THE STUPID BACON? I'M TALKING ABOUT THAT.
OH, THIS? IT'S A MAGIC LAMP.
8/31

DUDE...A MAGIC LAMP?! RUB IT, AND WE'LL MAKE THREE WISHES AND HAVE ANYTHING WE WANT IN THE WORLD!

HOPE YOU LIKE BACON.

HELLO. I AM CHI CHI PERÓN, PREACHER TO THE STARS. I HAVE BEEN PUT HERE ON EARTH TO JUDGE AND CONDEMN OTHERS.
LEAVE ME ALONE, RAT...

THROUGH THESE STATE-OF-THE-ART HEADPHONES, I RECEIVE DIVINE GUIDANCE AS TO WHO SHALL BE CONDEMNED TO A LIFE OF ETERNAL TORMENT.
HAVE YOU LOST YOUR 6#☆# MIND?
9/1

... I'VE GOT SOME BAD NEWS.

HELLO. I AM CHI CHI PERÓN, PREACHER TO THE STARS. I HAVE BEEN PUT HERE ON EARTH TO JUDGE AND CONDEMN OTHERS.
WHAT ARE YOU DOING, RAT?

I JUST TOLD YOU, MY SON. I AM CHI CHI PERÓN, AND THROUGH THESE HEADPHONES, I CAN HEAR THE VOICE OF GOD.
KNOCK IT OFF, RAT...IF GOD WAS GONNA SPEAK THROUGH SOMEONE, IT WOULDN'T BE YOU.
9/2

... GOD SAYS YOU'RE A BIG DUMB IDIOT AND THAT YOU SHOULD SHUT UP.
...TELL HIM TO SEND ME A SIGN, LIKE MAYBE A BURNING RAT.

Danny Donkey walked to school.
Danny Donkey saw Bob.
Bob called Danny a name.

Danny punched Bob.

Principal Jack saw Danny punch Bob.

Danny went to detention.

THIS IS THE CHILDREN'S BOOK YOU'VE BEEN WORKING ON?
YES. I SHOW FOOLISH BEHAVIOR AND HOPE KIDS LEARN FROM IT.

Only punch Bob when the principal is distracted.

I GOT A JOB WRITING ADS FOR A DOORKNOB COMPANY. I JUST WROTE MY FIRST ONE.
LET ME HEAR IT.

"IF YOU DON'T BUY OUR DOORKNOBS, GOD WON'T LOVE YOU, AND YOU'LL PROBABLY GO TO HELL."
9/4

ETERNAL CONDEMNATION IS THE KEY TO SELLING DOORKNOBS.

I HEAR YOU GOT A JOB WRITING ADS FOR A DOORKNOB COMPANY.
YEP. CHECK OUT THIS ONE.

"BUY OUR DOORKNOBS OR WE'LL BREAK YOUR G#☆G@#☆ KNEES."
9/5

THAT'S CALLED EXTORTION.
IT'S A FINE LINE.

AREN'T THESE MEERKATS AMAZING? ONE OF THEM ALWAYS KEEPS WATCH WHILE THE REST OF THEM SCURRY ABOUT IN THEIR UNDERGROUND TUNNELS.
ZOO

THAT'S SO CUTE... I WONDER WHAT THE REST OF THEM DO DOWN THERE WHILE HE KEEPS WATCH?
ZOO
9/6

XXX
MOONSHINE
MOON

WHAT ARE YOU DOING?
CALLING MY BOOKIE. I'M TAKING THE FORTY-NINERS AND THREE POINTS.

I THOUGHT THAT WAS ILLEGAL.
IT IS... BUT THESE GUYS HAVE BEEN RUNNING THEIR OPERATION FOR YEARS.

9/7

SO WHAT DO ALL THESE LITTLE MEERKATS DO?
WELL, GOAT SAYS THE ONE KEEPS WATCH WHILE THE REST OF THEM DIG UNDERGROUND TUNNELS.
ZOO

AWW... HOW CUTE... WOULDN'T YOU LOVE TO KNOW WHAT MOTIVATES AN INDUSTRIOUS L'IL GUY LIKE THAT?
ZOO

9/8
... AND REMEMBER, YOU NEVER MET ME.
GRACÍAS.
SAN DIEGO
TIJUANA

HEY, GOAT... GREAT NEWS! I'VE TAKEN THE LIBERTY OF TRACKING YOUR BLOG HITS AND THERE'S BEEN A TREMENDOUS UPTICK!
GO AWAY, RAT.
TYPE TYPE TYPE
9/9

YOU SEE, ON MONDAY, THERE WAS ONE HIT... THAT WAS ME. ON TUESDAY, THERE WAS ONE HIT... THAT WAS ALSO ME. BUT ON WEDNESDAY—LOOK OUT, MAMA—WE HAD A SURGE! TWO HITS!! WOO HOO HOOOOOOO!!!

OHHhhh... WAIT WAIT WAIT.. THAT WAS THE DAY MY BROWSER SHUT DOWN AND I HAD TO LOG BACK ON.

... MIND REIMBURSING ME FOR THE BALLOONS?

Hulloooooo, zeeba neighba... Leesten... Me need leetle help.

WHY DO YOU HAVE A WOOD CHIPPER ON YOUR FRONT LAWN?
Ohh, dat? Me just doing leetle yard work. But leesten, me tink me lose contakk lens.

WHERE'D YOU LOSE IT?
Me tink it at back of machine. But me no can reach.

GOSH, YOU KNOW.. MY ARMS JUST AREN'T LONG ENOUGH.. GUESS I WON'T BE ABLE TO FIND ——
HEY! Me got long arms! Me can find!!

BZZZZT

Does you find it?!

DID YOU PUT UP THESE 'LOST' POSTERS ALL OVER OUR CAFE'S BULLETIN BOARDS?
YES, SIR, I DID. IT'S A COMMUNITY SERVICE.. HELPS PEOPLE FIND THEIR LOST DOGS, CATS... WHY? IS THERE A PROBLEM?
Joe's

"LOST... MY BOSS' SOUL... SUCKED AWAY BY CORPORATE GREED."
Joe's
ROASTERY
9/11

YOU TAKE EVERYTHING SO PERSONAL.
Joe's
ROASTERY

HI... GIMME A TALL DECAF.
ROOM FOR CREAM?
Joe's
ROASTERY
9/12

YEAH.
HERE.
Joe's
ROASTERY

IT'S EMPTY.
HOPE YOU LIKE CREAM.
Joe's
ROASTERY

SIR, GOOD MORNING, SIR.. AT APPROXIMATELY 0300 LAST NIGHT, THREE TEENS IN A CAMARO THREW SOME LIT PICCOLO PETES INTO OUR TULIP BED.

AREN'T THOSE JUST FIREWORKS?
SIR, THESE THINGS CAN ESCALATE.
9/13

HOW DO YOU KNOW?

I ESCALATE THEM.
USA

HEY THERE, GOAT... LISTEN... ARE YOU A 'YANKEES' FAN?
NO. WHY?
TYPE TYPE TYPE

OH, IT WAS JUST THAT YOU AND YOUR BLOG REMINDED ME OF ALEX RODRIGUEZ YESTERDAY.
HOW SO?
TYPE TYPE TYPE
9/14

NEITHER OF YOU GOT ANY HITS.

WHY DO YOU ALWAYS LOOK SO UPSET?

GOODNIGHT, DAD.
Does you say you prayers?
9/15

NOT YET, DAD.
Okay. Let say togedder.
"Now me lay me down to sleep.
Mow da zeebas down like sheep.
Give dem to me nice and dead.
Me no happy 'Til me fed."

Goodnight, son.
I LOVE YOU, DAD.

WHAT ARE YOU DOING, PIG?
I'M LOOKING TO THE HEAVENS FOR ANSWERS TO LIFE'S DEEPEST MYSTERIES.

AND WHAT HAVE YOU FOUND?
THAT MOSQUITOS LIKE TO BITE MY RUMPUS.
9/16

I WAS HOPING FOR SOMETHING MORE PROFOUND.

HEY HEY HEY...WHO ARE YOU GUYS?

WE'RE FROM STARBICKS. WE'RE OPENING A CAFE IN YOUR LIVING ROOM.
WHOA WHOA WHOA YOU CAN'T DO THAT.

OH, REALLY? WHO'S GONNA STOP US?
THE COPS. I'LL CALL THE COPS. THEIR STATION'S RIGHT ACROSS THE STREET.

LOOK OUT YOUR WINDOW.

...IT'S A STARBICKS.

9/17

...MAYBE THEY'LL STILL LET US SLEEP HERE.
HEY! FELLAS! Y'MIND? I'M TRYING TO GET A LATTÉ.

Hulloooooo, zeeba neighba... Leesten... This my son. My hope is that he future killer of you.

9/18
FATHER, YOU KNOW THAT I'VE GIVEN IT A LOT OF THOUGHT AND THAT I'VE DECIDED THE MOST ETHICAL THING FOR ME TO DO IS TO BECOME A VEGETARIAN.

He a beeg disappointment.

Goobye, woomun. Me off try keel zeeba.
FATHER, HAVE YOU EVER CONSIDERED THAT THE ZEBRA MIGHT HAVE HIS OWN FAMILY?... A FAMILY THAT WOULD MISS HIM IF HE WERE GONE?

9/19

Mebbe he using drugs.

What is you doing, son?

READING ABOUT THE DANGERS OF EATING MEAT.
Reading big waste of time, son. Me no read. Look how smart me is.
9/20

GUESS WE CAN'T ALL BE BORN GENIUSES, POPS.
Dat gud point. Me special case.

LOOK, FATHER, THIS IS A PHOTO OF A CHICKEN RANCH. SEE HOW IN-HUMANE THE RANCHERS ARE?
Son son son... You sooo confused. We **muss** keel cheeckens.

WHY, FATHER? WHAT WOULD HAPPEN IF WE DIDN'T?

9/21
Dey keel **US**.

TELL ME I'M ADOPTED.

MOTHER....IS THERE ANY POSSIBILITY THAT I WAS SWITCHED AT BIRTH... i.e. THAT MY FATHER'S NOT MY FATHER?

9/22
NO, SON.

WHAT A BONE-CRUSHING BLOW TO MY PROSPECTS THAT IS.

NO OFFENSE, POPS.
Ohhhhkay... Say again, but slooooowly.

HI, THERE, RAT... MIND IF MY FRIEND, BOB, JOINS US FOR LUNCH TODAY? HE SHOULD BE HERE ANY MINUTE.
IS HE THAT GUY YOU SAID WAS THE VICTIM OF IDENTITY THEFT?

YEAH.... IT'S BEEN TOUGH FOR HIM.
OH, YEAH? HOW BIG OF A DEAL IS IT?

9/23
IT'S BIG.
HI, BOB.
BUMMER, DUDE.

WHAT ARE YOU DOING?
I JUST GOT A FAX FROM ZEBRA...BUT DON'T TOUCH IT..HE'S GOT A COLD.

WHAT ARE YOU TALKING ABOUT?
HIS GERMS ARE PROBABLY ON IT.

PIG..WHEN SOMEONE SENDS YOU A FAX, THEY'RE NOT SENDING YOU THE ACTUAL PIECE OF PAPER THEY WERE HOLDING.
YES THEY ARE.

THEN HOW COME WHEN YOU SEND A FAX, THE EXACT PAPER YOU "SENT" COMES OUT AT THE BOTTOM OF YOUR MACHINE?!
THAT'S A COPY...THE ORIGINAL FLIES MAGICALLY TO ZEBRA.

OH. BRILLIANT..THEN WHY DON'T YOU JUST SHOVE A HAM SANDWICH IN THERE? THAT WAY, ZEBRA'D GET ONE AND YOU'D GET ONE TOO...YOU STUPID @#☆@☆# PIG!!!!!
HAHAHA HAHAHA.. DON'T BE A SILLY-HEAD!

D'YOU GET IT?

HI... GIMME A DOUBLE DECAF LATTE.
NO.
Joe's ROASTERY

WHAT DO YOU MEAN, "NO"?
I'M ON BREAK.
Joe's ROASTERY

WHAT TIME'S YOUR BREAK END?
4:30.
Joe's ROASTERY

IT'S 9:15.
SWEET.
MAY I HAVE A WORD?
Joe's ROASTERY

HEY... ARE YOU GUYS GOING TO THE WATER PARK?
YEAH, DUDE, BUT I ONLY HAVE TWO TICKETS... YOU'LL HAVE TO AMUSE YOURSELF AT HOME.

WHIRRRRRRRRRRR

Hulloooooo, zeeba neighba... Me hear you getting alarm.
THAT'S RIGHT.

Ohhh... Dere no need for dat... We one big family.
YOU TRIED TO KILL ME IN MY SLEEP.

All family have probbums.

BEHOLD! THE PROTOTYPE OF MY "DANNY DONKEY" DOLL, A CUTE L'IL TALKING DOLL I HAD MADE IN CHINA... IT'S FOR KIDS OF ALL AGES.
HAHA IT'S SO HUGABLE!

GO AHEAD... PULL THE CORD AND HEAR IT SAY CUTE L'IL THINGS LIKE, "I LOVE LICORICE."
HAHAHA I'D LOVE TO.
PUUUUUULL
9/28
I ROB LIQUOR STORES. I ROB LIQUOR STORES.
IT APPEARS WE HAVE A TRANSLATION PROBLEM.
THERE'S NO BOOZE LIKE FREE BOOZE. THERE'S NO BOOZE LIKE FREE BOOZE.

YEAH... WHAT DO YOU WANT?
UHH, RAT... MAY I HAVE A WORD WITH YOU?
Joe's ROASTERY

9/29
WHAT IS IT?
LISTEN... YOU NEED TO START BEING FRIENDLIER WITH CUSTOMERS.. ..AND SMILE MORE.... THIS IS SUPPOSED TO BE A *HAPPY* PLACE.

YEAH... WHAT DO YOU WANT?

FORGET IT... JUST FORGET IT.
I AM SO @☆@#☆#@☆ HAPPY IT'S HARD TO BELIEVE.
Joe's ROASTERY

HELLO, MA'AM.. MAY I INTEREST YOU IN A TALKING "DANNY DONKEY" DOLL?... IT'S FOR KIDS OF ALL AGES.
WELL, I HAVE A YOUNG KID... WHAT'S IT SAY?
DANNY DONKEY

CUTE L'IL THINGS, LIKE "I LOVE HUGS," AND "I LOVE PUPPIES."... PULL THE CORD AND SEE FOR YOURSELF....
PUUULL
DANNY DONKEY

9/30
I DRINK BEER TO FORGET MY PROBLEMS. I DRINK BEER TO FORGET MY PROBLEMS.
DANNY DONKEY

WE'RE GETTING THAT FIXED!
DUDE, AM I LOADED! DUDE, AM I LOADED!
DANNY DONKEY

....AND THE SHELLING CONTINUED TODAY WITH NO APPARENT END IN—
CLICK

...FIRED TWO TEST MISSILES INTO—
CLICK

...THE PLOT, TO BLOW UP TEN COMMERCIAL FLIGHTS BETWEEN—
CLICK

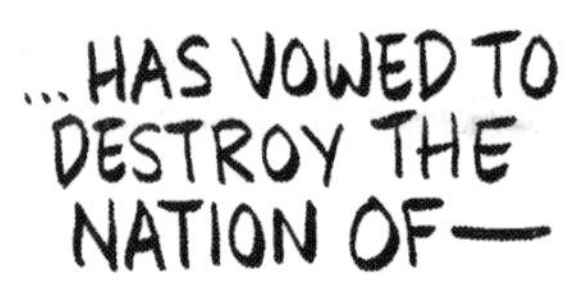
...HAS VOWED TO DESTROY THE NATION OF—

CLICK

...MAY BE WITHIN THREE YEARS OF DEVELOPING A NUCLEAR—
CLICK

10/1

HOPE YOU BROUGHT BEER.
End O'The World Box
BEER

HEY, HAVE YOU SEEN THE PROTOTYPE OF OF MY NEW "DANNY DONKEY" DOLL?
THE ONE YOU SHOWED ME YESTERDAY THAT SAYS, "I ROB LIQUOR STORES"?

YEAH. I HAVE TO SEND IT TO THE FACTORY SO THEY CAN MAKE IT SAY *APPROPRIATE* THINGS LIKE, "I LOVE RAINBOWS."
WELL, IT HAS TO BE AROUND HERE SOMEWHERE... HOW FAR COULD A CHILDREN'S STUFFED ANIMAL GET?
10/2

LIQUOR
CLOSED
6-PACK $5.99

WHAT ARE YOU READING?
"THE COMPLETE CALVIN AND HOBBES."... GOSH, I LOVE THIS COMIC STRIP.

WHAT DO YOU LIKE SO MUCH ABOUT IT?
THE FACT THAT YOU HAVE THIS STUFFED ANIMAL WHO COMES TO LIFE AND IS SO WISE AND KIND... WITH NEW COMICS SO EDGY AND DARK THESE DAYS, YOU GOTTA WONDER IF WE'LL EVER SEE A CHARACTER LIKE THAT AGAIN...
10/3

UUUURP...
CIGARETTES
BEER
BEER
BEER

I'M SAD... I JUST GOT THIS LETTER FROM MY MOM AND I THINK SHE SEES ME AS A BIG, FAT FAILURE.
PIG.. THAT'S A TERRIBLE THING TO SUGGEST... WHY WOULD YOU EVEN SAY THAT?

Pig,
You're a big, fat failure.
Mom
10/4

MAYBE I'M READING TOO MUCH INTO IT.

WHAT THE?... WHY'S MY "DANNY DONKEY" DOLL SURROUNDED BY BOOZE AND CIGARETTES? WHAT'D YOU DO?
I DIDN'T DO IT.
CIGARE

WELL, I DIDN'T DO IT.
THEN WHO DID?
CIGARE

CIGARE

OH, SURE... BLAME THE STUFFED ANIMAL.
CIGARE

PIG! THE COPS ARE HERE! THE DONKEY STOLE ALL THAT BEER AND THE COPS KNOW WE HAVE IT! QUICK! LET'S RAT HIM OUT!
YOU CAN'T DO THAT. I'M YOUR PAL.

WRONG, MORON... **PIG'S** MY PAL.. WE LOOK OUT FOR EACH OTHER.. WE SUPPORT EACH OTHER.. YOU'RE JUST A FELONIOUS DONKEY.. AND YOU'RE GOING **DOWN**!

I LOVE HUGS. I LOVE PUPPIES. I LOVE HUGS. I LOVE PUPPIES.

THE PIG DID IT.

HERE'S YOUR BURGER, AND HERE'S YOUR SALAD.
WHOA WHOA WHOA.. WHERE'S THE FRENCH DRESSING?

I DESPISE THIS COMIC STRIP.

Danny Donkey hated his neighbors.

He hated his doctor, his lawyer and his accountant.

He hated leaders, followers and florists.

He hated relatives, real estate agents, and relatives who were real estate agents.

"I must turn my hatred into something constructive," thought Danny Donkey. So Danny made a sign.

But no one listened.

So Danny hit them with his sign.

Suddenly realizing that the value of his sign was not in the message, but in the stick to which it was affixed, Danny spent the rest of his life hitting people with sticks.

WHAT ARE YOU READING?
"LEVITATING AND YOU: A STEP-BY-STEP GUIDE TO LEVITATION."

YOU STUPID FATHEAD... DO YOU REALLY THINK YOU CAN LEARN HOW TO LEVITATE FROM A BOOK?
WELL...NOT FROM CHAPTER ONE...IT'S JUST AN INTRODUCTION.
10/9

BUT CHAPTER TWO ROCKS.

PIG, THE POLICE ARE AT YOUR FRONT DOOR...I GUESS YOUR NEIGHBOR WAS TRYING TO SUNBATHE TOPLESS WHEN SHE SPOTTED SOMEONE LEVITATING OVER HER FENCE.

BUT I WOULD NEVER DO THAT. I DIDN'T STUDY A WHOLE BOOK ON LEVITATION JUST TO USE MY POWERS FOR EVIL...I SWEAR...
10/10

DON'T MIND ME.

ZEBRA? HI..I'M JANE. I UNDERSTAND YOU NEED A REAL ESTATE AGENT.
10/11

YEAH. I'M LOOKING TO SELL MY HOME.
WELL, IT LOOKS TO BE IN GOOD SHAPE...NICE LAWN...HOW ARE YOUR NEIGHBORS?

DIE! DIE! DIE! DIE!

WE HAVE ISSUES.

NOW, ZEBRA.. IF WE'RE GOING TO SELL YOUR HOUSE, WE NEED TO PRESENT IT IN THE BEST POSSIBLE LIGHT.
BUT I CAN'T DO ANYTHING ABOUT THE IDIOT CROCS. THEY'RE RIGHT NEXT DOOR.

I UNDERSTAND... BUT THAT MEANS WE'RE GONNA HAVE TO DO OUR VERY BEST TO MAKE SURE THAT AT LEAST EVERYTHING ELSE APPEARS NORMAL.

BAD TIME?

MR. PRESIDENT, THE WAR IN IRAQ HAS FORCED US TO MAKE SACRIFICES AT HOME... FOR ONE THING, OUR AIRSPACE STILL NEEDS TO BE SAFER.
HOW DO YOU FIGURE?

CALL SOMEONE.

WHO'S THAT GUY?
THAT'S ANGRY-CLIFF, THE MAN-SHEEP.

THE MAN-SHEEP?
YES. HALF-MAN. HALF-SHEEP. THE MAN PART HAS FREEDOM OF WILL, BUT THE SHEEP PART JUST FOLLOWS THE HERD. THIS CREATES INTERNAL CONFLICT. ...THUS, THE ANGER.

...DOES THIS STRIP REALLY APPEAR ON THE SAME PAGE AS "HI AND LOIS"?
YES. BUT WE HAVE TO KEEP A CERTAIN DISTANCE.

Angry Bob looked out his window and saw two little girls in green dresses going door-to-door with boxes of cookies.

"I can only assume those little girls are raising funds for their scouting organization," said Bob. "I will assist them by buying a box of cookies. Helping others will bring me happiness."

Eager to perform his act of kindness, Bob threw open his front door and skipped merrily toward the little girls.

"Oh, girls! Girls!" he shouted as he approached them from behind. Getting no response, he tapped one of them on the shoulder.

And heard a man scream. And heard two loud pops.

Falling, Bob saw the sign: "HELP AN ARMED, DEAF, EASILY-STARTLED, CROSS-DRESSING MIDGET GO TO SUMMER CAMP"

Ignominiously, Bob expired.

10/16

10/17

10/18

PSSST...PIG...IT'S ME, YOUR DUCK...MY CASTRO DISGUISE FAILED, SO I HAD TO HIDE INSIDE THIS "BOBO'S BURGER BOY" STATUE.

LISTEN...YOU NEED TO STOP RUNNING AROUND OUR NEIGHBORHOOD BLOWING UP PEOPLE'S MINIVANS... DO YOU UNDERSTAND ME?!
10/19

GET SOME HELP, SON.

I HEAR YOU'RE TRYING TO SELL YOUR HOUSE.
YEAH, BUT THE CROCS DON'T WANT ME TO. THEY WANT ME CLOSE WHERE THEY CAN KILL ME.

WHAT SAY DO THEY HAVE AS TO WHETHER YOU SELL YOUR HOUSE?
10/20

Bootiful place.
Yeah. Nutheeng exorceesm can't cure.
I'VE CHANGED MY MIND.

Achoo.

Oh no....Ees mold, asbestees and toxeec waste from nexx door affecteeng you allergies AGAIN?
10/21

Oh. No mind us.
FOR SALE

Ohhkay, zeeba neighba.. No more game. We crocs buy F-14 Supersoneecal jet...So geeve up or face conseekences.
SHOW ME THE PLANE.

Uh. Ees in backyard.
I CAN SEE YOUR BACKYARD. IT'S NOT THERE.
10/22

Ees behind trash can.
YEAH...THOSE PLANES ARE PROBABLY ABOUT TWENTY FEET HIGH..I DON'T THINK SO.

Ohhkay. FINE. You want truth, Meester Smart Guy?....Plane *inveesible*.
OHH..WELL.. I HADN'T CONSIDERED THAT. SO YOU CAN'T SEE IT EITHER?

NO. We no can.
SO EVEN IF YOU WANTED TO FLY IT, YOU COULDN'T BECAUSE YOU WOULDN'T BE ABLE TO FIND IT?

BINGO!! We no can fly NUTHeeng!!

Me was debater een high school.

WHAT ARE YOU DOING, RAT?
I'M BLIND JIMMY WINTHROP, BLUES SINGER FOR THE RICH.
BEER

THE BLUES ARE FOR PEOPLE WHO ARE DOWN AND OUT, PEOPLE WHO'VE LOST THEIR HOMES, THEIR JOBS, EVERYTHING THEY HAVE...
10/23

IT CAN BE PRETTY TOUGH WHEN 'NORDSTROMS' CLOSES EARLY.

WHAT ARE YOU DOING NOW, RAT?
I'M BLIND BOBBY Z., FOLK SINGER FOR THE RICH AND UPTRODDEN... CHECK OUT MY PROTEST SONG.

♫ HOOOOOW MANY ROADS MUST MY 'LEXUS' GO DOWN BEFOOOOOOORE THE ♫ WAAARRANTY ENDS... YES'N, HOOOOOOW MANY GAINS MUST MY STOCKBROKER MAKE BEFOOOOOOORE I CALL HIM MY FRIEND... ♫
10/24

GETS YOU RIGHT HERE.

♫ HOOOOOOOW MANY TIIIIMES ♫ MUST A D-O-O-O-LLAR BE TAXED BEFOOOOOORE I CAN CALLLLL IT ♫ MY OWN... ♪ ♫

YES'N, HOOOOOOW MANY BUUUCKS MUST THAT U-U-U-UNCLE SAM TAKE BEFOOOOOOORE I L-O-O-O-O-SE ♪ MY SUMMER HOME ♫ ♪
10/25

I CALL IT "MY CAPITAL GAINS ARE BLOWIN' AWAY IN THE WIND."
IT'S JUST SO SAD.
SNIFF SNIFF SNORT

HI...WHAT CAN I GET YOU TWO?
Geeve me steak... **RARE**....Me love blood....Me a true predeetor!... HAHAHAHAAA...

AND I'LL HAVE A SMALL SALAD AND YOUR VEGGIE BUR
LALALALALALALALA LALALALALALALALA LALALALALALALALA LALALA
10/26

REAL MATURE, DAD.
Dad? Dad? Who dis 'dad' you speek of ??

SIR, A CONFIDENTIAL SOURCE INFORMS ME THAT YOUR NEIGHBORS ARE PLANNING TO THREATEN YOU.
IS THAT SO?

YES. THE PLAN IS TO EXTORT CONCESSIONS. TO TAKE WHAT IS NOT THEIRS. THEY'VE EVEN GIVEN IT A CODE NAME...
10/27

"HALLOWEEN."

I ADMIRE YOUR COOLNESS UNDER FIRE, SIR.

SIR, GOOD EVENING, SIR....SIR, A SECOND SOURCE HAS CONFIRMED THAT YOUR NEIGHBORS ARE PLANNING AN INVASION OF OUR PERIMETER. THEY SHALL BE DISGUISED.

IT'S CALLED "HALLOWEEN," LITTLE DUCK, AND I'M GONNA GIVE THEM ALL THE CANDY THEY WANT.
IT'S CALLED "APPEASEMENT," SIR, AND ALL MILITARY HISTORY COUNSELS AGAINST IT. ASK NEVILLE CHAMBERLAIN.
10/28

THE NICE MAN WHO SCORED ALL THOSE BASKETS?
THAT'S WILT, SIR, BUT YOU'RE CLOSE.

TRICK OR TREAT!!
Hullooo, keeds. Hahaha... Dat gud deesguise.

Here you goes.
SPLORT

EWWW.
GROSS.
SICK.
WHAT IS THAT?

Antylope brain. Me got extra.

AAAAHHHHHH
10/29

Spoiled keeds.
Nexx year we turn off porch light.

I HEAR YOUR DUCK WAS AGAINST GIVING OUT CANDY TO TRICK-OR-TREATERS.
YES. HE CALLS IT 'APPEASEMENT.' BUT HE CALMED DOWN WHEN I TOLD HIM HE COULD GO TRICK-OR-TREATING HIMSELF.

YOU'RE LETTING HIM TRICK-OR-TREAT?
OH, SURE, BUT I MADE HIM PROMISE HE'D BE POLITE AND RESPECTFUL.

FORK IT OVER, BIG DADDY!!

TRICK OR TREAT!
LOOK, HONEY. A CUTE L'IL DONKEY! GIVE HIM SOME CANDY!
WHAT KIND WOULD YOU LIKE, L'IL GUY?

BOOZE. SO I CAN FORGET MY TROUBLES.

HERE...JUST POUR IT IN THE PUMPKIN.
LET'S TURN OFF THE PORCH LIGHT NOW, SWEETIE.

I AM GOING TO RUN FOR MAYOR. MY CAMPAIGN WILL CENTER AROUND FEAR.
FEAR OF WHAT?

RAINBOWS. DEADLY RAINBOWS.
BUT RAINBOWS AREN'T DEADLY.

I SEE YOU'RE SOFT ON RAINBOWS.

SIR.. WE UNDERSTAND YOU'RE CENTERING YOUR CAMPAIGN ON THE THREAT POSED BY RAINBOWS.. BUT HOW DO YOU KNOW RAINBOWS ARE DEADLY?
FOR THAT, I'LL TURN TO MY DIRECTOR OF INTELLIGENCE, PIG, WHO HAS INCONTROVERTIBLE PHOTOGRAPHIC PROOF.

Ahhh
HAHA HAA
11/2

I'M CONVINCED.
GOOD ENOUGH FOR ME.
LET'S HIT THE BAR, BOYS.
THANKS FOR COMING!

BAD NEWS... YOUR RUN FOR MAYOR IS NO LONGER UNOPPOSED.

WHAT?! WHO'S RUNNING AGAINST ME?!... WHAT'S HIS PLATFORM?!
11/3

Keel tings.

THE CROC'S MAYORAL CAMPAIGN
SIR, EVERYONE KNOWS WHAT YOU WANT TO DO WITH THE ZEBRAS, BUT WHERE DO YOU STAND ON OTHER ISSUES?... FOR EXAMPLE, WHAT WOULD YOU DO ABOUT ILLEGAL ALIENS?

Eat da slow ones.
11/4

I'M SENSING A PATTERN.
Heeeeey... Meester fat reporter... You looking niiiiiiiiiiiice....

HI..WHAT DO YOU WANT?
I'D LIKE A REALLY LARGE COFFEE, SO... ...UH...GIVE ME THE 'TALL.'
Joe's ROASTERY

THAT'S THE SMALL.
'TALL' IS SMALL?

TALL IS SMALL.
SO WHAT'S 'GRANDE'?
Joe's ROASTERY

'GRANDE' MEANS 'LARGE'.
THEN GIVE ME A 'GRANDE.'
Joe's

BUT HERE IT MEANS 'MEDIUM.'
WHAT THE?! DUDE, ALL I WANT IS A LARGE COFFEE!
Joe's

THEN ORDER A 'VENTI.'
SO 'VENTI' MEANS 'LARGE'?!

NO, 'VENTI' MEANS 'TWENTY,' AS IN, "I JUST SPENT TWENTY MINUTES TRYING TO UNDERSTAND A MENU."

AAAUUGHHH
I THINK I'M REALLY STARTING TO ENJOY THIS JOB.

THE MAYORAL DEBATES
MY OPPONENT IS SOFT ON RAINBOWS!
My opponenn make friend wid edible aneemals!!

MY OPPONENT WEARS THONG UNDERWEAR WITH TINY LITTLE RAINBOWS ALL OVER THEM!!
HA! Me no even WEAR Undywear! LOOK!!

...SEE...THIS IS WHY I DON'T VOTE.
HAHAHA...NO UNDERWEAR! HE'S GOT HIM THERE!

BAD NEWS... THE ELECTION FOR MAYOR IS MOOT.
MOOT?! HOW CAN IT BE MOOT?

THERE'S BEEN A COUP.
A COUP?! WHO THE HECK WOULD LAUNCH A STUPID COUP FOR THE MAYOR'S OFFICE?!

COULD SOMEONE PLEASE BRING ME MY 'ENEMIES LIST'?

I BELIEVE YOUR SUCCESS IN LIFE IS DETERMINED BY THE NUMBER OF HITS YOU GET WHEN YOU 'GOOGLE' YOUR OWN NAME...NOT SURPRISINGLY, A SEARCH FOR 'RAT' AND 'PEARLS BEFORE SWINE' PRODUCES A WHOPPING 71,500 HITS...

HAHAHA...WHAT A FUNNY COINCIDENCE, BECAUSE JUST YESTERDAY, I THOUGHT I'D HAVE SOME FUN, SO I 'GOOGLED' 'PIG' AND 'PEARLS BEFORE SWINE' AND GOT 112,000 HITS!...ISN'T THAT THE SILLIEST THING?

YOUR EGO IS OUT OF CONTROL.

11/9

11/10

11/11

Months ago, 'Pearls' creator Stephan Pastis determined that one of his crocodile characters, Biff, was simply too dumb and delusional to live with the other crocodiles in the Zeeba Zeeba Eata Fraternity house. Thus, Stephan moved Biff into his own backyard, where he could care for him. We now rejoin the comic, already in progress.

(Editor's Note: Due to a pagination error, the dialogue from today's Pearls Before Swine has been inadvertently omitted. From the limited portion that is viewable, it appears that the angry nun in panel (3) is scolding an inebriated monkey. For those of you who may be inconvenienced by the omission, we'd like to remind you that the angry nun/drunken monkey gag is about as hackneyed as one could imagine in contemporary comedy, and probably offered very little in the way of humor value. Thank you for your patience.)

WHAT ARE YOU DOING NOW?
I'M WRITING A STUPID LETTER APOLOGIZIN TO THE GU WHO LAYS OU THE NEWSPAPE COMICS PAG
DON'T CALL ME TOOTSIE ROLL.
THEN DON'T CALL ME LUCKY CHARM.
darb
WHY?? YOU IDN'T DO ANY- THING JRONG.
I KNOW! I KNOW! BUT THIS GUY'S JUST KNOCKING OUT OUR PANELS AND REPLACING 'EM WITH RANDOM 'GET FUZZY' PANELS!
HAHAHA! I *LOVE* THAT CLUELESS SATCHEL!! HAHAHA HAHAHA
HA... HA...... HEH... ......HA.............. ....OH.
I DON'T *FEEL* LIKE I'M CLUELESS...
11/16

NO, NO, NO. IT'S **ON**. AND THIS TIME... IT'S MARSUPIAL.
I GUESS THE POINT IS THAT IT'S ON.
HOLD THE PHONE... THIS SAYS "SOMEONE WILL GIVE YOU A LARGE SUM OF MONEY." ...SCORE.
WILL YOU PLEASE APOLOGIZE TO THE GUY WHO LAYS OUT THE NEWSPAPER COMICS PAGE SO THAT HE'LL STOP FILLING OUR SPACE WITH RANDOM 'GET FUZZY' PANELS?
I DID! I EVEN SENT HIM A CASE OF BEER.
GOOD. 'CAUSE I ACTUALLY MET THAT GUY ONCE AND I KNOW THAT HE *REALLY* LOVES THAT "REDTAIL ALE" STUFF... I HOPE THAT'S WHAT YOU SENT... I MEAN, I HOPE YOU DIDN'T CHEAP OUT AND JUST SEND HIM ONE OF THOSE MASS-MARKETED GENERIC BRANDS...
I'LL BE IN THE KITCHEN ~~EATING A CAN OF RAISINS~~. not drinking cheap beer.
11/17

HEY! WE GOT OUR STRIP BACK!
YEAH. THE GUY WHO LAYS OUT THE COMICS PROMISED THAT AS LONG AS I WATCH IT WITH THE INSULTS, HE'LL LEAVE OUR STRIP ALONE.

NO HAVING THE STRIP SLIP? NO PRINTING 'GET FUZZY' PANELS? NO COMPRESSING THE IMAGE?
NOPE. I'LL BE GOOD AND DO MY JOB AND IN TURN, HE'LL BE GOOD AND DO WHATEVER IT IS A USELESS CRETIN LIKE HIM DOES...

MY, YOU'VE GROWN FAT.
11/18

Banana dog fig face
Banana dog fig face
Banana dog fig face
HOSANNA!

HELLO, NEIGHBOR FLOYD...AS YOU MAY KNOW, I BECAME MAYOR IN A MILITARY COUP. SADLY, YOU'RE ON MY ENEMIES LIST.

SO WHAT?
11/20

WELL, I WANT TO BE A NICE GUY, FLOYD, SO IF YOU'LL JUST PROMISE TO BE A GOOD NEIGHBOR, I'LL TAKE YOU OFF THE LIST...OTHERWISE, I HAVE TO CALL FOR AIR SUPPORT.

I DON'T THINK YOU KNOW WHO YOU'RE MESSING WITH, YOU

YOU MAKE POOR CHOICES, FLOYD.

DAD...HOW DID YOU KNOW WHEN YOU FIRST LOVED MOM?
11/21

Eet was bootiful night. Full moon. We sat by lake and watch bootiful swans sweem by.
DID YOU KISS HER?

No. She too busy killing swans.

HOW ROMANTIC.
Eet was love at first death roll.

LOOKS LIKE 'PEARLS' FINISHED SIXTEENTH OUT OF TWENTY STRIPS IN THIS NEWSPAPER'S COMICS POLL....THE OVER-65 VOTE IS JUST KILLING YOU.
'PEARLS' CARTOONIST STEPHAN PASTIS
11/22

WHAT DO YOU WANT ME TO DO? DRAW A STRIP LIKE 'PICKLES' ABOUT A COUPLE OF OLDER PEOPLE JUST TO PICK UP VOTES?
'PICKLES' FINISHED FIRST.

I LOST MY GLASSES, OPAL.
CHECK YOUR FACE, EARL.

I KNOW YOU SAW MY BOMB SHELTER, FLOYD, AND I WANT YOU TO KNOW RIGHT NOW THAT IF THE END OF THE WORLD COMES, I'M NOT LETTING YOU IN IT.

11/25

HIYA, RAT.

WHAT'S THAT YOU'RE DOING WITH YOUR HAND?
IT'S HOW I INDICATE "HI" OR "BYE," DUDE.. I NOTICED ON 'ENTERTAINMENT TONIGHT' THAT NONE OF THE COOL HOLLYWOOD TYPES EVER ACTUALLY **SAY** "HI" OR "BYE"... THEY JUST MAKE THE PEACE SYMBOL.
11/26

BUT YOU'RE STICKING OUT YOUR THUMB, TOO.
I KNOW... THAT'S MY SPECIAL TOUCH.. BY ADDING AN EXTRA DIGIT, MY GESTURE IS 50% COOLER THAN THEIR GESTURE... AND IT'S HECKA COOLER THAN YOUR DUMB "HIYA."

YOU DO IT LIKE THIS?
DUDE.. THAT DOES NOT MEAN **YOU** CAN USE IT.. THIS IS FOR COOL PEOPLE. YOU'RE BARELY A THIRD OF MY COOL.

THEN WHAT CAN I DO?
WELL, IF I'M ENTITLED TO THREE FINGERS, I'LL GRACIOUSLY PERMIT YOU ONE.

OKAY... HOW'S THIS?

HEY.. WHAT THE @#☆#'s THAT SUPPOSED TO MEAN YOU @#☆#@#☆ PIG?... *I'LL TEACH YOU TO—*
SMACK
SMACK
POW

...STICK WITH 'HIYA.'

You wanted see us, Meester Cartoonist?
YEAH, LISTEN...I'M THINKING OF SENDING YOU ALL OUT ON A SECRET MISSION AROUND THE COUNTRY.
S. PASTIS

11/27
Seecret meeshun? Niiiiice! I like! But why you need so many of us?
WELL, I REALLY ONLY NEED ONE OR TWO OF YOU, BUT AT THE RATE YOU GUYS DIE, I THOUGHT I'D BRING EXTRA.

Which one of us 'extra'?
Oh! Peeck me! Peeck me!
S. PASTIS

So, meester cartoonist, What is seecret meeshun you send us on?
I WANT YOU TO GO AROUND THE COUNTRY AND FIND ALL THE SENSITIVE FOLK WHO GET OFFENDED AT SOMETHING THEY SEE IN A COMIC STRIP.
S. PASTIS

And inTEEMidate dem wid fierce set of choppers?!?
S. PASTIS

11/28
DUDE. HAVE A 'TIC TAC.'
Oooh...Red pill or blue pill...Juss like 'Matrix.'
S. PASTIS

OKAY GUYS, LISTEN..YOUR JOB IS TO FIND ALL THE FOLKS WHO TAKE OFFENSE AT A COMIC STRIP AND SHOW THEM HOW TAME NEWSPAPER COMICS ARE COMPARED TO CARTOONS ON T.V.
S. PASTIS

11/29
SO SHOW 'EM THIS "SIMPSONS" D.V.D.
Me LOVE dem!
THEN SOME "FAMILY GUY."
Dey GREAT!
THEN THIS "SOUTH PARK."
Heelarius!
THEN MY BOOK.
PEARLS

CRICKETS
You steenk.
Yeah. You no "Mark Trail."

So you want us crocs go around country and find people who get ohfended at comeecs?
YES.
But how we find dem?
11/30

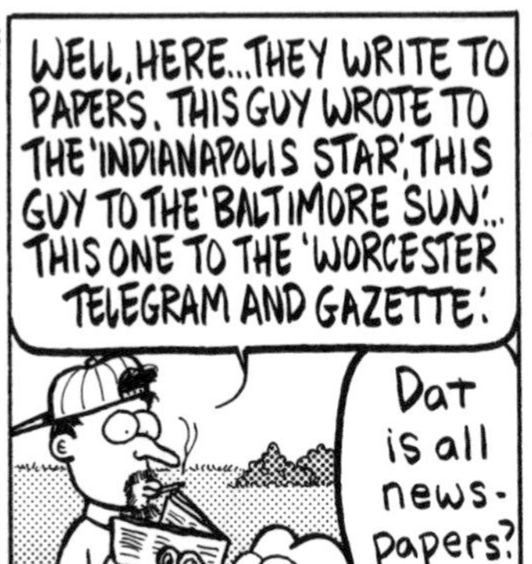
WELL, HERE...THEY WRITE TO PAPERS. THIS GUY WROTE TO THE 'INDIANAPOLIS STAR', THIS GUY TO THE 'BALTIMORE SUN'... THIS ONE TO THE 'WORCESTER TELEGRAM AND GAZETTE'.
Dat is all news-papers?

THEY'RE NOT *JUST* NEWSPAPERS...THEY'RE *TERRIFIC* NEWSPAPERS WITH REALLY BRIGHT EDITORS AND GREAT PUBLISHERS.

FOR SHAME, YOU PITIFUL SUCK-UP.
STAY OUT OF THIS.
HAHA. Pasties is booty kisser.

Hullooo, gud person...Leesten. We unnerstand you write letter to paper complaining of 'Pearls in Swine' and praising 'Snuffy Smith.'
12/1

THAT'S RIGHT. I *LOVE* 'SNUFFY SMITH'.....AND MY FATHER LOVED 'SNUFFY SMITH.'

ONE HOUR LATER...
...AND MY FATHER'S FATHER'S FATHER'S FATHER'S FATHER'S FATHER'S FATHER LOVED 'SNUFFY SMITH.'...AND MY....
ZZZZZZZZZ

WHAT'S THAT YOU'RE SIGNING, CHRIS?
JOE'S ROASTERY CHRISTMAS CARDS...ALL OF US EMPLOYEES SIGN THEM AND THEY SEND THEM TO OUR BEST CUSTOMERS.
Joe's ROASTERY

DO *I* HAVE TO SIGN THEM?
'FRAID SO, RAT.
Joe's ROASTERY
12/2

"MERRY BLAH BLAH BLAH BITE ME."
THAT'S NOT VERY CHRISTMASY.

DON'T SAY THAT, L'IL GUARD DUCK! I'LL HELP YOU! BUT FIRST WE'RE GONNA CHEER YOU UP! WHAT WOULD YOU LIKE TO DO? GO TO THE PARK?... PLAY SOME FRISBEE? GET SOME ICE CREAM?

Story Update: 'Pearls Before Swine' cartoonist Stephan Pastis has sent his crocs on a mission to find and appease comic strip readers from coast to coast. We rejoin the story, already in progress.

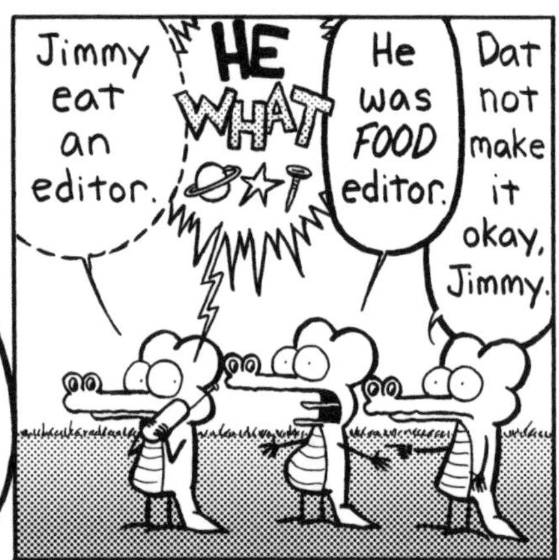

WELL, I JUST GOT OFF THE PHONE WITH MY SURGEON. LOOKS LIKE THEY'LL BE ABLE TO RE-ATTACH MY DRAWING ARM TOMORROW.
Dat great!
12/7

Yeah. Mebbe in meantime, we glue on, so you can draw streep.
NO NEED. PART OF BEING A SYNDICATED CARTOONIST MEANS KNOWING HOW TO DRAW WITH EITHER HAND.

TELL ME AGAIN HOW HE GOT SYNDICATED.

I'M DIVIDING ALL OF HUMANITY INTO TWO LISTS, WHICH I'M CALLING, 'PEOPLE I DON'T LIKE,' AND 'PEOPLE I CAN'T STAND.'

OH, THAT'S VERY CYNICAL, RAT... YOU NEED TO MAKE A THIRD LIST OF PEOPLE YOU LIKE AND GIVE IT A NICE LITTLE TITLE.
HMM... YOU'RE RIGHT...
12/8

Future Disappointments

THOSE STUPID BIRDS NAILED MY CAR AGAIN.
OHH... THEY DON'T MEAN ANY HARM. THEY'RE JUST BEING BIRDS.

THAT'S WHAT I KEEP TELLING MYSELF, BUT I SWEAR, WITH THE AMOUNT OF TIMES THEY NAIL IT, YOU'D THINK THEY WERE SOME FREAKY BIRD FRATERNITY TURNING THEIR BIRD-DROPPING SKILL INTO SOME WARPED FRAT GAME.
DON'T YOU THINK YOU'RE BEING A LITTLE PARANOID?
12/9

DANG! THAT'S THREE IN A ROW FOR BOB... LOOKS LIKE LARRY HERE'S GOTTA DRINK AGAIN!
I GOTTA UUURP... WHUUU ???
DRINK! DRINK! DRINK!

Gladys sat alone on a grassy hill, her jet black hair waving gently in the breeze.

A tall, manly stranger approached. "I am Bob," he said, in a tall manly way.

Their eyes met. Her heart raced. Her goose pimples got goose pimply.

Bob took her in his muscular arms. They kissed. They did more than kiss.

It was love. Passionate. Fierce. White hot.

And on a glorious moonlit night, they were wed.
12/10

And spent the next 41 years watching TV in separate recliners.

YOU REALLY SHOULDN'T BE WRITING ROMANCE NOVELS.
He grabbed for the remote. She slapped his face.

DON'T YOU HATE IT WHEN YOU'RE ON A HIGHWAY WITH ONE LANE AND THE SLOW DRIVER IN FRONT OF YOU WON'T PULL OVER, NO MATTER *HOW* MANY CARS ARE LINED UP BEHIND HIM?
I DO.

WELL, I THINK I'VE FOUND A PRACTICAL SOLUTION...IT'S CALLED 'THE OPEN HIGHWAY FACILITATOR.'
HOW'S IT WORK?

YOU PRETTY MUCH JUST PULL THE TRIGGER.
DO *NOT* SELL HIM WEAPONS.
HE *SAID* HE'D BE RESPONSIBLE.

HEY, GOAT, WHERE WERE YOU TODAY?
I WENT TO A PETRIFIED FOREST. THEY HAVE THESE TREES THAT ARE SO OLD THEY ACTUALLY TURNED TO STONE.

AWWW. HOW SAD.
WHY IS THAT SAD?

BECAUSE I THINK THAT HAPPENED TO MY GRANDMOTHER.

NEVER MIND.
POOR OL' GRANDMA.

HI...GIMME A SOY MILK CAPPUCCINO.
SORRY... NOT IN THE MOOD.
Joe's ROASTERY

NOT IN THE *MOOD*?
YEAH, NOT IN THE MOOD. YOU KNOW, LIKE YOUR WIFE WHEN YOU ASK HER FOR S
Joe's ROASTERY

SSSSSSSSSSSSSSSOY MILK CAPPUCCINO.... ...ON THE HOUSE, SIR.
Mmmph
Joe's ROASTERY

...AND REALLY, YOU HAVE TO ASK YOURSELF, AT THE END OF THE DAY, WHAT DOES IT REALLY MATTER?

I'M SORRY, BUT DID YOU JUST USE THE EXPRESSION, "AT THE END OF THE DAY"?
YES. YES, I DID.
12/14

WHAM
WHAM
WHAM

I'M GONNA STOP THAT EXPRESSION ONE SPEAKER AT A TIME.

12/15
PUSH
BUTTON
FOR
PUSH
PUSH

WHAT DO YOU WANT?
UH... NOTHING. I WAS JUST TRYING TO CROSS.
THEN WHAT THE G#G# ARE YOU BOTHERING ME FOR?

I GOTTA START READING THESE THINGS.

WHAT'S THAT THING?
IT'S MY SECURITY MONKEY. LINUS HAD HIS BLUE BLANKET... I HAVE MY TOY MONKEY... WHENEVER SOMEONE MAKES ME FEEL BAD, I JUST TURN ON MY MONKEY AND IT MAKES ME FEEL GOOD.

Y'KNOW, THAT MIGHT BE CUTE FOR A LITTLE KID, BUT FOR SOMEONE GROWN UP LIKE YOU, THAT'S EMBARRASSING... NOT TO MENTION SAD....
12/16

CLANG
CLANG
CLANG
CLANG
CLANG
CLANG
CLANG
CLANG
CLANG

OKAY, GUYS, EVERYBODY SMILE!
I HATE THESE STUPID CHRISTMAS CARD PHOTOS.

THUD!

OH, BOY! IT'S ONE OF SANTA'S ELVES! I BET HE'S HERE TO PICK UP OUR LISTS FOR SANTA! I GOTTA GET MY LIST FOR SANTA!
12/17

UURRRRP

OH, THAT IS SOOO NOT IN THE SPIRIT OF CHRISTMAS.

Ho ho hooo zeeba neighba... Come sit on Santa lap. Tell Santa what you want get for Keesmas. Santa give to you anyting.

I'D LIKE A WORLD WHERE I CAN BE SAFE IN MY OWN BACKYARD... A WORLD WHERE NO ONE TRIES TO EAT ME... A WORLD WHERE I CAN LIVE IN PEACE.
12/18

How 'bout nice train?

SIR, RELIGIOUS ZEALOTS HAVE TAKEN OVER THE STREETS... IT'S A MOB SCENE... PEOPLE WITH FUNNY HEAD COVERINGS... THE CHANTING OF FUNDAMENTALIST DOGMA.. CALL RETREAT, SIR.. THE GREAT HOLY WAR IS UPON US.

"AWAY IN A MANGER NO CRIB FOR HIS BED... THE LITTLE LORD JESUS LAID DOWN HIS SWEET HEAD."
12/19
CAROLS
CAROLS

LEMME GUESS. THEY PUT A FATWA ON THE DUCK.

12/20

NO.
Nuts.

MERRY CHRISTMAS, ZEEBA NEIGHBA!
WOW... A PICTURE OF THE SERENGETI! THANK YOU, LITTLE GUY!

YEAH, IT'S TO REMIND YOU OF YOUR FELLOW ZEBRAS LIVING OUT ON THE PLAINS...THAT WAY YOU WON'T GET HOMESICK.
THAT'S SURE NICE OF YOU.... YOU SURE YOUR DAD WON'T MIND?
12/21

Dear Santa,
Save us from destruction.
Save us from war.
Save us from ourselves.

YOU STUPID PIG... SANTA SPECIALIZES IN TOYS...HE GIVES TOYS.
12/22

Please throw in a yo-yo.

This year my greatness was startling.

I made more cash than you.
I bought nicer things than you.
I had more success than you.

In short, here is my summary of the last twelve months.
Me: Total domination.
You: Blah blah blah who cares?
12/23

YOU REALLY SHOULDN'T SEND OUT AN ANNUAL CHRISTMAS LETTER.

Deer Santy Closs,
You know what me Want....
Black and white. Four legs.
Two beeg ears. Super stoopid.
P.S. You grate!!

12/24

MERRY CHRISTMAS, PIG... I DIDN'T BUY YOU ANYTHING, BUT I THOUGHT I COULD GIVE YOU ONE OF THESE...

AWW, GEE, LITTLE BUDDY, THAT MEANS MORE TO ME THAN ANY-THING. I JUST GOT YOU A LITTLE GIFT CERTIFICATE. HERE, IT'S IN MY...

12/25
COULD I HAVE MY WALLET BACK?
Dang.

I HOPE YOU DON'T MIND, BUT I TOLD OUR NEIGHBORS WE WOULD BABYSIT THEIR ONE-YEAR-OLD SON WHILE THEY GO OUT TO DINNER.
DUDE... TELL ME YOU'RE KIDDING. I *HATE* BABIES.

OHH, IT WON'T BE SO BAD.... I HEAR HE'S VERY ADVANCED FOR HIS AGE.
PLEASE.... HOW ADVANCED CAN A ONE-YEAR-OLD BE?
12/26

SPORTSCENTER... *NOW.*

HEY, NEIGHBOR PHIL... WHAT ARE YOU UP TO?
THE ANCIENT ART OF FAL-CONRY, PIG... AFTER RAISING MY LOYAL AND BELOVED FALCONS FOR SIX YEARS, I HAVE LET THEM GO.

AND NOW... I AWAIT THEIR RETURN... THE GLORIOUS AND WONDROUS HIGH POINT IN ANY TRUE FALCONER'S LIFE.
12/27

TO FREEDOM.
TO PHIL BEING A BIG, FAT IDIOT.

CAN I HELP YOU, SIR?
YES. I NEED A GUN. MY NEIGHBOR BOTHERS ME AND I'D LIKE TO POP HIM IN THE REAR A COUPLE OF TIMES.
WALMARTOPIALAND GUNS

SIR...I CAN'T SELL A GUN TO SOMEONE WHO TELLS ME THAT THEY'RE GONNA "POP" THEIR NEIGHBOR IN THE REAR "A COUPLE OF TIMES."
FINE. I TAKE IT BACK... I SHALL ONLY SHOOT HIM ONCE.

... CURSE THESE LIBERAL GUN LAWS.

CAN I HELP YOU, SIR?
YES. I'D LIKE A GUN SO I CAN POP MY NEIGHBOR IN THE REAR.................. ...HE BOTHERS ME.
WALMARTOPIALAND GUNS

SIR, I CAN'T—
OKAY, STOP RIGHT THERE, YOU DENNIS KUCINICH-LOVING LIBERAL... I HOLD IN MY HANDS A COPY OF THE SECOND AMENDMENT TO OUR CONSTITUTION, WHICH STATES AS FOLLOWS, "IT SHALL BE THE RIGHT OF ALL AMERICANS TO SHOOT THEIR NEIGHBOR IN THE @#*."

HE DIDN'T FALL FOR IT.

CAN I HELP YOU, SIR?
YES, I'D LIKE TO BUY A GUN TO SHOOT................ ....BIRDS!..... GEESE, TO BE EXACT.
WALMARTOPIALAND GUNS

OKAY, FINE... THERE IS, HOWEVER, A FIVE-DAY WAITING PERIOD TO—
WHAT?!? I CAN'T WAIT THAT LONG!! I'M MAD **NOW** AT MY STUPID..............GOOSE... HE'S BEEN A BAD..... GOOSE.... ...REAL BAD....

HE'S ON TO ME.

GUARD DUCK, THIS IS MAURA. SHE'S A GIRL DUCK...I'M HOPING THAT HAVING A GIRL AROUND WILL HELP CALM YOU DOWN.

HOW DO YOU DO, MA'AM?
QUACK
SIR...THIS IS A NON-ANTHROPOMORPHIC DUCK, SIR.
A WHAT?

SIR, I'M ANTHROPOMORPHIC...THAT MEANS I'VE TAKEN ON THE CHARACTERISTICS OF A HUMAN BEING...SEE HOW I TALK AND WEAR A HELMET?.... THIS GIRL'S JUST A DUCK.
AND DOES THAT MATTER?
12/31

I'M AFRAID IT DOES, PIG.
STEPHAN PASTIS? CREATOR OF 'PEARLS'?

HI, PIG..YEAH, LISTEN.. YOU CAN'T INTRODUCE A NON-ANTHRO ANIMAL INTO THE STRIP...THEY HAVE TO BE ABLE TO TALK AND STUFF...IT'S PART OF THE PREMISE.
I'M SORRY, MR. PASTIS. PLEASE DON'T FIRE ME!

PIG, PIG, PIG... RELAX, BUDDY... YOU'RE THE LEAST OF MY PROBLEMS. BELIEVE ME, I'VE GOT CHARACTERS WHO—

WELL WELL WELL... IF IT'S NOT MR. "I GUESS GOOD ART IS NO LONGER A REQUIREMENT FOR THE COMICS PAGE."
I GOTTA GO.
IT'S OKAY, STEPHAN, YOU'VE GOT A NICE PERSONALITY.

WHO'S YOUR FRIEND THERE, GUARD DUCK?
MAURA, THE NON-ANTHROPOMORPHIC DUCK..THAT MEANS SHE CAN'T TALK OR ANYTHING... SHE'S JUST A DUCK.

1/1
IS SHE GOING TO BE A REGULAR CHARACTER?
NO. THE STRIP'S CREATOR, STEPHAN PASTIS, SAYS THAT ALL ANIMALS IN THE STRIP HAVE TO BE ABLE TO TALK AND STUFF... AND RULES ARE RULES.

KISS

PERHAPS WE'RE BEING TOO STRICT.
ASTIS

YOU KNOW, MAURA, AT FIRST I THOUGHT YOUR INABILITY TO TALK WOULD HAMPER OUR RE-LATIONSHIP... BUT NOW I SEE THERE ARE ADVANTAGES...

1/2
FOR INSTANCE, YOU CAN NEVER TELL ME TO TURN OFF THE GAME OR EMPTY THE TRASH... AND WHEN YOU DO MAKE SOUNDS, THEY'RE ALL OPEN TO INTERPRETATION.
QUAAACK

YOU DON'T HAVE TO KEEP SAYING, 'YOU HOT STUD,' AFTER ALL MY SENTENCES.

HEY... I HEAR THAT GUARD DUCK IS DATING A NON-ANTHROPOMORPHIC DUCK. I THOUGHT YOU SAID HE COULDN'T DO THAT.
S. PASTIS

1/3
I CHANGED MY MIND... I THOUGHT OF A FEW JOKES I COULD DO WITH HER.
S. PASTIS
IT MUST BE SORT OF HARD TO BE A CARTOONIST WITH SUCH LIMITED ABILITIES... SORT OF LIKE A BASKET-BALL PLAYER WITH NO ARMS...... OR LEGS...... .... OR HEAD....
S. PASTIS

I **GET** THE ANALOGY.
...JUST A LONELY TORSO ROLLING AROUND THE HALF COURT LINE.
S. PASTIS

HELLO, SIR...I'D LIKE TO GET THE CHATEAUBRIAND, COOKED MEDIUM WELL, AND A GLASS OF YOUR FINEST PINOT NOIR.
WONDERFUL...AND FOR THE LADY?

1/4
SHE'S GOING OUTSIDE TO EAT BUGS.

SHE'S JUST A DUCK.

HI, MAURA...THESE FLOWERS ARE FOR YOU...I THINK I LOVE YOU...PLEASE DON'T LEAVE ME...PLEASE DON'T DISAPPOINT ME LIKE EVERYONE ELSE IN MY LIFE.

1/5
QUACK
QUACK
QUACK
QUACK
QUACK
QUACK

NEVER PIN YOUR HOPES ON A MIGRATORY BIRD.

CAN I HELP— OH, GREAT... YOU AGAIN...
PLEASE, SIR...DO NOT PREJUDGE ME...I WOULD LIKE TO PURCHASE A GUN IN ORDER TO PREVENT CRIME.
WALMARTOPIALAND
GUNS

1/6
OH?...AND WHAT CRIME IS THAT?
THE CRIME OF MY BREAKING INTO YOUR ESTABLISHMENT LATE AT NIGHT TO STEAL A GUN THAT AN IDIOT NAMED YOU REFUSED TO SELL ME LEGALLY.

SO MUCH FOR THE DIPLOMATIC APPROACH.

Larry... What you doing?
Me is tree-climbing assassin monkey.

Larry... You juss crockydile.
Haha.. **You** know me crockydile. ***Me*** know me crockydile. But zeeba not know nutheeng.

You tink ?
Me *know*...Zeeba juss over fence...He at birthday party for neighba's keed. When he leave, me pounce.

And dat work?
Of course dat work...Once zeeba see he in jaws of tree-climbing assassin monkey, he geeve up so fast dat —

WHAM
1/7
Ohhh... SORRY, KIDS.. LOOKS LIKE THE PIÑATA'S OVER *HERE*.
GOOD...THIS ONE'S A RIP-OFF.
GIMME CANDY! CANDY! CANDY!

1/8
RUMBLE RUMBLE RUMBLE
KSSHH!!
ONE REFRIGERATOR MAGNET TOO MANY.

WHO'S YOUR TALL FRIEND?
ATATURK, THE LLAMA. HE'S A DIPLOMAT.

A DIPLOMAT? HOW WONDERFUL! SO WHAT'S HIS METHOD FOR HANDLING DISPUTES? FRIENDLY MEETINGS? BUILDING TRUST? MAKING COMPROMISES?

1/9
PTUI

I PREFER FRIENDLY MEETINGS.

WHAT'S WRONG WITH YOUR FRIEND?
ATATURK THE LLAMA IS SAD BECAUSE HE'S BEEN KICKED OUT OF THE U.N. FOR SPITTING ON OTHER DIPLOMATS.

WELL, MAYBE LLAMAS SHOULD STOP SPITTING... IT IS KIND OF A GROSS HABIT.

1/10
SPITOOO

THE LLAMA NATION DENOUNCES YOUR CULTURAL INSENSITIVITY.

HEY, PAL...SHOOT A BASKET, WIN A PRIZE...JUST THREE BUCKS.
WHAT ARE YOU DOING, RAT?

I'VE TURNED OUR BACKYARD INTO A TRAVELING CARNIVAL. I THOUGHT IT'D BE FUN.
YOU'RE NOT JUST DOING IT TO TAKE PEOPLE'S MONEY?

WHAT'S THAT SUPPOSED TO MEAN?

WHAT'S THE MOST IMPORTANT THING IN LIFE, DAD? IS IT LOVE? HAPPINESS? IS IT HELPING OTHERS?

Leesten, son... Most important ting in life ees to find udders who in beeg trubble and need you help...
WHY IS THAT, DAD?

Because dey is da ones you eat.

THANKS ANYWAYS, DAD.
Me always here to help, son.

WHERE WERE YOU TODAY?
I WENT TO THE FURNITURE STORE TO BUY A NIGHT STAND...I ALREADY HAVE ONE ON ONE SIDE OF MY BED, AND I'D LIKE TO PUT ONE ON THE OTHER.

I'M SORRY, BUT I COULDN'T HELP OVERHEARING...DID YOU SAY YOU'RE LOOKING FOR A NIGHTLIGHT? IF SO, I WORK FOR A LAMP STORE AND I'D LOVE TO SELL YOU SOMETHING...
UHH...NO, I'M JUST LOOKING FOR...UHH.... ONE NIGHT STAND.

...GUESS I SHOULD HAVE BOUGHT A LAMP...

...And den if Floyd attack dis way and Bob attack from dis way....

1/14

WHAT ARE YOU DOING, LARRY?
Woomun, peese! Dis serious plan of bissness. Is you stoopid?

OOOOH, SO THIS IS A STRATEGY SESSION??
You beleeve dis, Floyd? Dis what me have put up wiff.

GIMME A BREAK, LARRY! YOU HAVEN'T CAUGHT A THING IN THREE YEARS!
Ohhkay, fat mouf! You want know?! Me tell! Farmer down street buy rooster! Ees black. Ees smart. And we is gonna KEEL!

THAT'S A WEATHERVANE, LARRY. IT'S NOT ALIVE.

Dis changes plan.

BEHOLD... MY LATEST DEVICE..THE "BLASTFROMTHEPASTOMETER"... IT ALLOWS YOU TO GO BACK TO ANY DATE IN HISTORY AND GRAB ANY PERSON YOU WANT OUT OF THAT ERA.
1865
The Blastfromthepast ometer

WHY WOULD YOU WANT TO DO THAT?
TO SHOW THEM THE PRESENT DAY, AND ALL OF OUR MODERN TECHNOLOGICAL ADVANCES.
LIKE WHAT?
1865
The Blastfromthepast ometer

CHIPS IN A CAN... WHO'DA THUNK IT?

SO HOW'S LIFE BACK IN D.C.?
AWFUL. THERE'S THIS BIG WAR AND MY WIFE'S A PAIN IN THE REAR.

HOW SO?
WELL, FOR EXAMPLE, RIGHT NOW SHE'S GOT THESE TICKETS TO A PLAY, AND I *HATE* PLAYS, BUT SHE SAYS I HAVE TO GO.

YOU REALLY DISLIKE PLAYS?
DISLIKE 'EM?... I'LL TELL YOU, I NEED TO SEE A PLAY LIKE I NEED A HOLE IN THE HEAD.

(AWKWARD SILENCE)

WHAT ARE YOU DOING, LINCOLN?
I HAVE TO WRITE THIS STUPID SPEECH AND I'M STRUGGLING WITH THE OPENING.

LET'S HEAR IT.
"FOUR SCORE AND SEVEN YEARS AGO, OUR FATHERS BROUGHT FORTH UPON THIS CONTINENT A NEW NATION."

YEAH. VERY BORING. TRY THIS.

"A LONG TIME AGO, IN A GALAXY FAR, FAR AWAY, A GREAT ADVENTURE TOOK PLACE."

BAD NEWS. LINCOLN WAS WATCHING "THE HISTORY CHANNEL" AND FOUND OUT HE GETS ASSASSINATED DURING THE MIDDLE OF A PLAY.

OH, NO. WHAT DO WE DO?
WELL, HE'S REALLY BUMMED, SO TRY TO MAKE HIM FEEL BETTER.
1/18

WELL, IF YOU'VE SEEN ONE PLAY, YOU'VE SEEN 'EM ALL.

WELL, GENTLEMEN.... I'M GOING BACK HOME.
BUT WHAT ABOUT WHAT HAPPENS AT THE PLAY?
CHOMP CHOMP
1/19

I'M GONNA DUCK... I'VE BEEN WORKING ON MY REFLEXES... GO AHEAD... THROW THAT BANANA AT ME...

SMACK

@☆#@.

Okay, zeeba neighba... Geev up now, because you is doomed. But no take my word for it. Leesten Miss Croco, who look deep in magic crystal ball and geev you future.
1/20

"Brunswick, 16 lbs."

You need start coming to meetings.

TOOT TOOOOT
WHAT ARE YOU GUYS DOING?
Train to Nowhere

IT'S THE 'TRAIN TO NOWHERE.' AND THAT'S 'DOOMSDAY, THE WONDER DOG'... HOP ON BOARD!
WHY WOULD I TAKE A TRAIN TO NOWHERE?
Train to Nowhere

BECAUSE THE TRAIN TO NOWHERE IS BASED ON THE THEORY THAT ANYWHERE IS BETTER THAN HERE... AND GIVEN THE PRESENT STATE OF THE WORLD, WE THINK THAT'S PRETTY APT.

YOU CAN'T DO THAT... EACH ONE OF US HAS A DUTY TO STAY AND DO EVERYTHING WE CAN TO HELP... TO WORK FOR THE BENEFIT OF OTHERS. ... NOT TO RUN AND FLEE...

Train to Nowhere

I FELT SORTA BAD RUNNING OVER HIS TOES.
YAH! YAH!
Train to Nowhere

PIG'S GOING BACK TO SCHOOL.
DOES HE WANT TO GET HIS COLLEGE DEGREE?

I THINK THAT'S A WAYS OFF.
WHY DO YOU SAY THAT?

JIMMY'S NOT KEEPING HIS HANDS TO HIMSELF.
CAT
DOG

MY GIRL LEFT ME.
HEY, SORRY TO HEAR THAT, PAL. THAT HAPPENED TO ME A COUPLE MONTHS BACK. WHAT WAS IT...ANOTHER GUY?

WINTER.

JUST WHEN YOU THINK YOU KNOW A GIRL.

Hulloooooo, leetle guard duck...Hey, We hear you got probbums.
Snicker
Snicker
Snicker
SNOOOORT

Ohhhh, me dunno... like mebbe you girlfriend, she.....FLY AWAY!!
HAHAHAHA Dat Frank is da greatest!!

FIVE MINUTES LATER...
But he make nice pair of boots, too.
Frank! Frank! Say someting!

1/27

WHEN THE RUSSIANS COME POURING OVER OUR NORTHERN BORDER BRINGING THE LATEST IN MILITARY HARDWARE, *DON'T COME CRYIN' TO ME,* 'CAUSE I WILL NOT BE THERE TO DEFEND YOUR HAPPY, LITTLE LIBERAL WAY OF LIFE.

HAVE YOU NOTICED HOW MANY PEOPLE ARE NOW ADDING BIG FRONT PORCHES TO THEIR HOUSES?
WHAT FOR?

I DUNNO... I GUESS IT ENCOURAGES NEIGHBORS TO COME UP AND CHAT...

YEAH... A BUNCH OF OUR NEIGHBORS ARE ADDING THEM... OUR BLOCK'S LIKE ONE BIG SOCIAL GATHERING!...

ISN'T IT FUNNY THAT AFTER ALL THESE YEARS OF BUILDING LARGER AND LARGER HOUSES TO HIDE FROM ONE ANOTHER, EVERYONE NOW DISCOVERS THEY MISS OTHER PEOPLE?

WELL... NOT EVERYONE.

MORNIN', RAT.
KEEP IT MOVING, BOB.

WHY DO YOU HAVE A SPAGHETTI STRAINER ON YOUR HEAD?

BECAUSE MY BASEBALL CAP IS DIRTY.

1/31

MY FIG TREE?? YOU WANT TO COMPLAIN ABOUT MY FIG TREE? OKAY, I'VE GOT A GRIEVANCE... ...MY NEIGHBORS TRY TO KILL ME SO THEY CAN EAT MY HEAD!

Betty sat alone by the wind-swept airfield.
She was sad.
She was lonely.

She came here to dream.
To watch the planes land.
To imagine the distant lovers reunited by these giant graceful birds of steel.

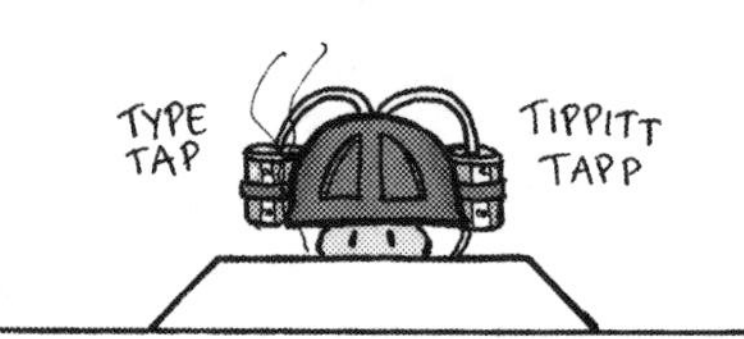

A stranger approached.
"I am Bob," he said.
He was tall and tan with muscular arms.

Their eyes met.
They kissed.
They did more than kiss.

TIPPITY TAP TYPE TAP

It was love.
White hot and fierce.

A dirigible floated just overhead. "That is as my love for you," Bob said. "Large, steady, sure and true."

And the Hindenburg exploded.

TYPE TYPE

TYPE TYPE

DID YOU HEAR ONE OF THE CROCS MOVED TO KANSAS CITY?
KANSAS CITY? WHY KANSAS CITY?

HE GOT A JOB WRITING SYMPATHY CARDS FOR HALLMARK.
WHAT'S A PREDATOR KNOW ABOUT COMFORTING SOMEONE WHO'S JUST LOST A FAMILY MEMBER?

"NOW DERE MORE FOOD FOR DA REST OF YOU"?
Dat very comforteeng.

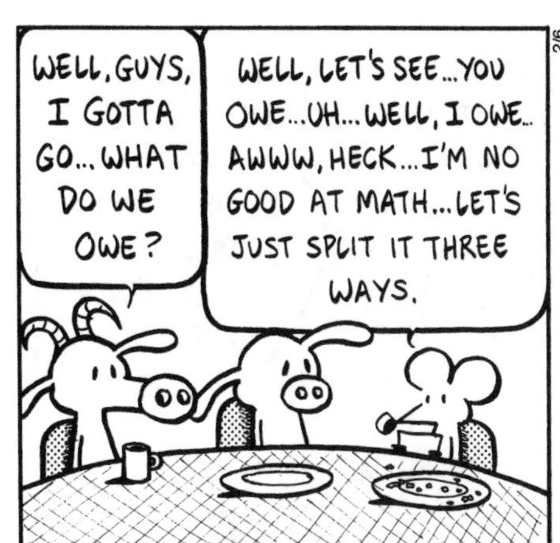
WELL, GUYS, I GOTTA GO... WHAT DO WE OWE?
WELL, LET'S SEE...YOU OWE...UH...WELL, I OWE.. AWWW, HECK...I'M NO GOOD AT MATH...LET'S JUST SPLIT IT THREE WAYS.

I HAD COFFEE. YOU HAD LOBSTER.

SOMETIMES IT PAYS TO BE NO GOOD AT MATH.

HALLMARK™ HEADQUARTERS: ANNIVERSARY CARD WRITING DIVISION
ALRIGHT, PEOPLE, WE WANT TO AVOID TRITE SUPERFICIALITY WITH THESE CARDS...GIVE US SOMETHING HEARTFELT...SOMETHING HONEST...

Happy anniversey, You big fat Pain in butt.

TOO MUCH.

THIS PAINTING REALLY SPEAKS TO ME.
WHY IS THAT?
MUSEUM

BECAUSE HE'S A SAD, LONELY FOOL AND I PITY HIM.
MUSEUM

AND YOU SHOULD HEAR THE FRAME.
USEUM

ISN'T IT ODD THAT WE ALL HAVE TO ACT LIKE WE LIVE NORMAL LIVES WHEN IN TRUTH WE ALL KNOW THAT ONE DAY HUMANITY WILL MOST LIKELY BLOW ITSELF UP?... I MEAN, AREN'T WE ALL JUST WHISTLING PAST THE GRAVEYARD?
NOT ME.

WHY NOT YOU?
I CAN'T WHISTLE.

...MAYBE YOUR DESTRUCTION'S NOT SUCH A BAD THING.
AND IF I COULD WHISTLE, I SURE WOULDN'T WASTE IT ON ENTERTAINING THE DEAD... THEY, LIKE, ALMOST NEVER APPLAUD.

DAD, DO YOU EVER THINK THAT THE KILLING OF ANOTHER LIVING THING IS IMMORAL?... THAT MAYBE THE DESTRUCTION OF A ZEBRA, EVEN FOR SUS-TENANCE, IS A SIN?

Leesten, son... You juss remembah one ting.

Every time a zeeba die, an angel get his wings.

I DON'T THINK THAT'S HOW IT GOES, DAD.
Ees a wunnerful life, son.

HEY... LISTEN TO THIS RIDDLE I JUST READ.
OHH, GOODIE.. I'M GREAT AT RIDDLES.

A MAN HAS A FOX, A CHICKEN, AND SOME CORN. HE HAS TO TAKE THEM ALL ACROSS A RIVER. HE CAN ONLY TAKE ONE OF THE ITEMS AT A TIME IN HIS BOAT.

HOWEVER, IF HE LEAVES THE FOX ALONE WITH THE CHICKEN, THE FOX WILL EAT THE CHICKEN. IF HE LEAVES THE CHICKEN ALONE WITH THE CORN, THE CHICKEN WILL EAT THE CORN.

WHAT SHOULD HE DO?

BUY A BIGGER BOAT.

IT'S NOT THAT HARD IF YOU THINK ABOUT IT.

2/12
WHERE YOU GOING WITH THOSE ROLLS OF QUARTERS?
SUPERMARKET. I HAVE TO DO OUR WEEKLY SHOPPING.

WHY DO YOU NEED TO PAY WITH CHANGE? THERE'S A TWENTY SITTING ON THE KITCHEN TABLE.
NO REASON.

2/13
I GOT A BOX OF CANDY HEARTS FROM A SECRET ADMIRER... YOU KNOW, THE ONES WITH WORDS PRINTED ON THEM?
OH, THAT'S SO ROMANTIC... READ ME ONE.

"Be my fud."

Someone no like his seecret mirerer.
Dat guy break my heart.

2/14
Dear Maura,
It is Valentine's Day. And I miss you.

From now on, I will only become attached to things that cannot migrate.

SQUEEZE

I just hugged my beer can.

I'M LEAVING YOU, PIG.
2/15

WHY?
YOU'RE A WIMP. I WANT A BOY-FRIEND WHO'S THE TOUGH, OUTDOORSY TYPE. I WANT A MANLY MAN.

BUT THAT'S ME.
PROVE IT.

HAHAHA...YEAH...AND THEN I BLAH BLAH BLAH BLAH BLAH BLAH AND SHE'S LIKE, BLAH BLAH BLAH BLAH BLAH BLAH BLAH....
Joe's ROASTERY

ANYHOOOOoo...I BETTER GET GOING...GOTTA GET MY MORNING CAFFEINE RUSH..HEHHEHHEH....YOU TAKE CARE NOW...BYE NOW...
Beep Beep Boop Beep Beep
Joe's ROASTERY
2/16

HI... GIVE ME A—
PIG? WHAZZUUUUUP? IT'S ME, RAT... OH, NOTHING.... JUST WAITING ON SOME LARDBUTT WHO WOULDN'T GET OFF HIS @#%@ CELL PHONE...
Joe's

WILL YOU PLEASE—
YEAH, HE'S STILL STAND-ING THERE.... WHO KNOWS WHY?...MAYBE THE LARDBUTT THINKS HE'S GETTING COFFEE... ANYHOOOOoo.....
Joe's

OUR CARTOONIST, STEPHAN PASTIS, IS SICK TODAY, SO HE ASKED US TO JUST LOOK THROUGH HIS JOKE FILE AND PICK A JOKE TO READ.
HOW 'BOUT THAT ONE?
Jokes
2/17

OKAY...UH..."HEY, DID YOU HEAR THERE WAS A FIRE AT THE USED CLOTHING STORE AND TWO PEOPLE DIED IN THE BUILDING NEXT DOOR?"
"NO...HOW'D THEY DIE?"
"SECONDHAND SMOKE."

LET'S KEEP LOOKING.
LET'S.
Jokes

HEY THERE, RAY... I HEARD YOU AND YOUR BROTHER HUGH GOT JOBS AT THAT NEW FAST FOOD PLACE DOWN-TOWN... HOW'S IT GOING?
RAY

NOT TOO GOOD, PIG... OUR BOSS WANTS THE TWO OF US TO KEEP A COUNT OF HOW MANY CUSTOMERS WE SERVE PER HOUR... THE HIGHER OUR COMBINED TOTAL, THE HIGHER OUR BONUS.
RAY

WHAT'S WRONG WITH THAT?
WELL, MY COUNT'S REAL HIGH, BUT HUGH IS SUPER SLOW... HE'S GONNA LOSE US OUR BONUS.
2-18
RAY

SO WHAT ARE YOU GONNA DO?
WHAT **CAN** I DO? I WANT MY BONUS AND I WANT HUGH TO GET HIS BONUS, SO I GUESS I'M GONNA HAVE TO JUST DOUBLE MY CUSTOMER COUNT.
RAY

THAT'S ASKING TOO MUCH OF YOURSELF, RAY.
THEN WHAT SHOULD I DO?

ASK NOT WHAT YOUR COUNT, RAY, CAN DO FOR HUGH... ASK WHAT HUGH CAN DO FOR YOUR COUNT, RAY.
RAY

YOU SHOULD BE ASHAMED.
S. PASTIS

HEY DAD..WOULD YOU MIND READING ME SOME NURSERY RHYMES?
Sure ting, son.

Jack be nimble
Jack be quick...

Kill dat man
He make me sick.

PLEASE DON'T CHANGE THE WORDS.
But dis Jack very annoying.

SIR, WE'VE GOT A SITUATION, SIR. A COMPANY OF UNIFORMED COMBATANTS IS ATTEMPTING TO EXTORT FUNDS...REQUEST PERMISSION TO ENGAGE, SIR.

COOKIES

FOR SHAME, SIR.
COOKIES
COOKIES

HEY THERE, GOAT...THIS IS MY NEW DOLL, 'MANIC DEPRESSIVE BARBINA.'... YOU'LL HAVE TO EXCUSE HER RIGHT NOW...SHE'S GOING THROUGH ONE OF HER LOW PHASES.

'MANIC DEPRESSIVE BARBINA'?.. WHAT THE...? HOW DO YOU EVEN KNOW WHEN SHE'S—
I'M SORRY... CAN YOU EXCUSE ME FOR A SECOND?

PLEASE STOP PAINTING YOUR MALIBU BEACH HOUSE BLACK.

2/22

TO MY GOOD BUDDY BILL... YOU'RE ALREADY MISSED.

2/23

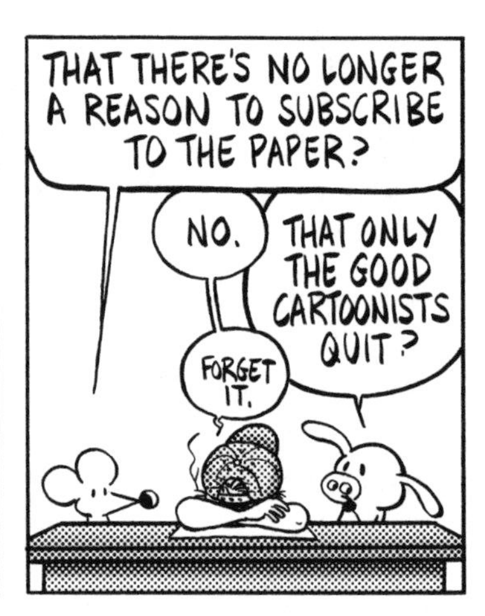

2/24

WHERE'S ALL THE TOFU I BOUGHT, MOM?

WHAT IS IT, MOM?
OH, SON, I WAS HOPING TO WAIT AND TELL YOU THIS WHEN YOU WERE OLDER....

WHAT IS IT? AM I ADOPTED? ARE YOU AND DAD SPLITTING UP?
WORSE, SON... YOUR FATHER BELIEVES IN THE TOFU COW.

THE WHAT?

SON, YOUR FATHER BELIEVES THAT TOFU IS A MEAT THAT COMES FROM THE MIGHTY TOFU COW. IF YOU PUT TOFU IN THE FRIDGE, HE WILL SCULPT IT INTO A TOFU COW, PUT IT OUTSIDE AND CONVINCE HIMSELF IT'S REAL.

WHY, MOTHER, WHY?
BECAUSE HE THINKS *I* BELIEVE IN THE TOFU COW, SON... AND WHEN HE CATCHES IT, HE FEELS PROUD.

CATCHES IT?!... MOTHER, TELL ME MY DAD DOESN'T HUNT—

WOE TO DA TOFU COW!!
NO NO NO NOO NO NOO
DON'T LOOK, SON... DON'T LOOK.
2/25

HEY, WHAT'S THE MATTER WITH YOUR FRIEND?
Oh, heem? He choking.
ACK!

2/26
AREN'T YOU GONNA HELP?
Oh, no... Death of fellow predator mean less competeetion for prey.
THUD

YOU GUYS ARE *COLD*.
Hey, look. Me got footstool.

DID YOU EVER WONDER WHY THE LETTERS ON A COMPUTER KEYBOARD ARE NOT ARRANGED ALPHABETICALLY? THE ANSWER DATES BACK TO THE DAYS OF MANUAL TYPEWRITERS.

2/27
COMMONLY USED COMBINATIONS OF LETTERS HAD TO BE PLACED FAR APART ON THE KEYBOARD TO PREVENT THEIR METAL KEYS FROM JAMMING TOGETHER WHEN THE TYPIST TYPED FAST.

IT'S A WONDER YOU DON'T GET MORE DATES.

WHAT'S WRONG WITH YOUR FRIEND?
Oh, he have bad heart. Probbly heart attack.
Ack.

2/28
AREN'T YOU GONNA HELP?
Why he need help to have heart attack?

YOU PREDATORS ARE JUST EVIL.
Ooooooooh. New hat.

WHOA. THAT BOAT'S ABOUT TO GO OVER THE EDGE.
THE EDGE OF WHAT?
3/1

THE WORLD THERE.
THE WORLD'S ROUND, PIG.

SO IS MY KITCHEN TABLE, BUT YOU CAN STILL KNOCK OFF THE CEREAL BOWL.

I GUESS 'SORRY' ISN'T IN YOUR VOCABULARY.

OUR SEWING MACHINE KEEPS ACTING UP... IT'S LIKE IT'S POSSESSED OR SOMETHING.
HOW COME EVERY TIME A STUPID APPLIANCE ACTS UP, PEOPLE SAY IT'S "POSSESSED"?

I LOVE SATAN. I LOVE SATAN.
3/2

CALL A PRIEST.

I CAN'T BELIEVE OUR SEWING MACHINE IS POSSESSED.
I CAN'T BELIEVE IT EITHER... IT RAISES SO MANY DEEP, MIND-BLOWING, PHILOSOPHICAL QUESTIONS.
3/3

LIKE WHAT?

LIKE WHY DO TWO ANIMALS WHO DON'T WEAR CLOTHES OWN A SEWING MACHINE?

...AND SO...IF YOU JUST..UH..MEET ME ...LIKE..UHH.....AT THE UHH...

WHAT ARE YOU UP TO, RAT?

LISTENING TO THIS IDIOT'S ENDLESS MESSAGE..ALL I WANT IS FOR HIM TO SAY HIS STUPID PHONE NUMBER.
SOOOOOO ANYHOO...

YEAH I HATE THAT... IT'S—
WAIT WAIT WAIT.. SHUT UP... I THINK HE'S ABOUT TO SAY IT...
SO...UH...GIVE..UH ME...A...CALL...UH ...THE NUMBER...IS

TWO!!

WHY ARE THE SLOWEST MESSAGE TALKERS THE FASTEST PHONE NUMBER GIVERS?
'CAUSE PEOPLE ARE MORONS!! MORONS!! MORONS!!
BAM
BAM
BAM

THE CROCODILE WAITS BELOW THE SURFACE OF THE POND. HE KNOWS THAT THIS IS THE ZEBRA'S ONLY SOURCE OF WATER.

AS THE ZEBRA LEANS IN TO DRINK, THE CROC STRIKES.... THE ZEBRA IS NO MORE.

3/5

HI THERE. I DON'T BELIEVE WE'VE MET. I'M PIG.
HI. TIMMY THE ANTEATER.
3/6

ANTEATER, HUH?...SO WHAT DO WHAT DO THOSE LITTLE GUYS TASTE LIKE?
WHAT DO WHAT LITTLE GUYS TASTE LIKE?

ANTS.
HOW THE @#☆@ WOULD I KNOW? I EAT MOSTACCIOLI.

SORRY.
I COULD DO WITHOUT THE RACIAL PROFILING.

PIG BOUGHT A POLE FROM THAT GENTLEMAN'S CLUB THAT SHUT DOWN.
A POLE? YOU MEAN ONE OF THOSE THINGS THAT SCANTILY CLAD WOMEN DANCE AROUND?
3/7

YEAH. AND HE'S HAVING IT INSTALLED IN OUR LIVING ROOM.
WOW...OUR OWN SWEET PIG...I CAN'T IMAGINE WHY HE'D EVER DO SUCH A THING.

INDOOR TETHERBALL: A DREAM COME TRUE.

WHATSA MATTER WITH YOU?
DEPRESSION FINALLY GOT THE BETTER OF OUR POOR LITTLE SOAP.

3/8
WHAT ARE YOU TALKING ABOUT?
HE HUNG HIMSELF IN THE SHOWER.

THAT'S CALLED "SOAP ON A ROPE."

THIS IS NO TIME FOR POETRY.

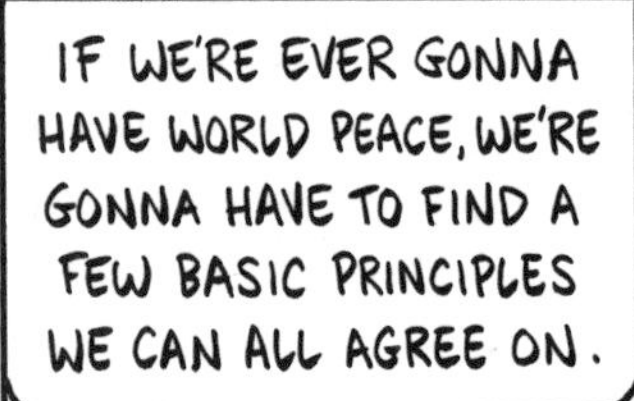
IF WE'RE EVER GONNA HAVE WORLD PEACE, WE'RE GONNA HAVE TO FIND A FEW BASIC PRINCIPLES WE CAN ALL AGREE ON.

3/9
THAT'S A VERY MATURE THING FOR YOU TO SAY, RAT. WHAT KIND OF PRINCIPLE DO YOU THINK WE COULD ALL AGREE ON?

THAT GUYS WHO WEAR THEIR COLLAR UP SHOULD ALL BE PUNCHED IN THE HEAD.

Ohhhhhhhhhhhhhh Lord...
HEY...WHAT'S A LITTLE VIOLENCE WHEN YOUR GOAL IS WORLD PEACE?
WE SHOULD GO HOME NOW, DEAR.

GOAT, I'D LIKE YOU TO MEET MY COUSINS. THIS IS BOB AND THAT'S GLADYS.

3/10
WHAT'S GLADYS DOING WAY OUT THERE?

SHE'S A DISTANT RELATIVE.

THAT'S CLOSE ENOUGH, GLADYS!

WHO'S YOUR WEIRD-LOOKING FRIEND?
EURIPEDES, THE ONE-EYED FROG.

WHAT HAPPENED TO HIS EYE?
NOTHING. HE JUST KEEPS IT CLOSED.

WHY WOULD HE KEEP ONE EYE CLOSED?
BECAUSE EURIPEDES BELIEVES THAT THE WORLD IS FILLED WITH PAIN. BY CLOSING ONE EYE, HE SHUTS OUT HALF OF IT.

BUT AREN'T THERE DISADVANTAGES TO ONLY SEEING OUT OF HIS LEFT EYE?
WELL, HE HAS NO DEPTH PERCEPTION, SO HE CAN'T PLAY CATCH, BUT OTHER THAN THAT, I CAN'T THINK OF ANY.

CLOMP

I THOUGHT OF ONE.
3/11

WHAT ARE YOU DOING, RAT?
I STOLE SOME STEM CELLS AND BEGAN CREATING MY VERY OWN HUMAN BEING FROM THE GROUND UP.

BUT THOSE ARE JUST FEET.

I GOT BORED.

HEY THERE, NEIGHBOR NICOLETTE, HOW GOES IT?
NOT GOOD, PIG... MY HUSBAND AND I HAVE BEEN TRYING FOREVER TO HAVE KIDS, BUT SO FAR, NO LUCK... OHH, HOW I LONG FOR THE PITTER PATTER OF LITTLE FEET...

PITTER PATTER
PITTER PATTER
PITTER PATTER

HAVE YOU SEEN....?

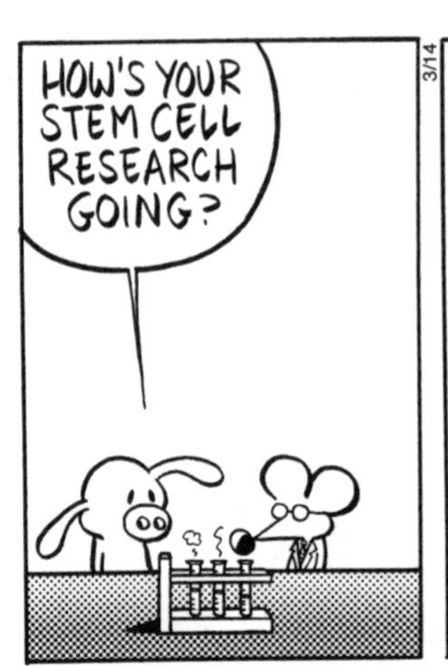
HOW'S YOUR STEM CELL RESEARCH GOING?

PRETTY GOOD.
JUST FINE.
SWELL.
PEACHY.

SUDDENLY, I'M VERY AGAINST CLONING.
OHH
THAT'S
NOT
NICE
YOU FATHEAD.

HEY, WHAT'S THE MATTER WITH YOU, GOAT?
I'M JUST IN A BAD MOOD AND DON'T FEEL LIKE DEALING WITH ANYONE.

3/15
HIYA!

THIS DOESN'T BODE WELL.

ALRIGHT, GUYS, IF I'M GONNA HAVE LITTLE CLONES RUNNING AROUND, I NEED TO BE SURE YOU UNDERSTAND RATSONIAN IDEOLOGY... THUS, PLEASE READ THE FOLLOWING QUESTION...

People are:
A) Kind.
B) Loving.
C) Big fat idiots to be distrusted and loathed.
"B"

WHAM

3/16
THAT WAS INCORRECT.

HEY THERE, PIG... HOW'D YOU SLEEP LAST NIGHT?
OH, PRETTY GOOD, RAT.. THANKS FOR ASKING.

3/17
CAN I BUY YOU A CUP OF JOE?
OH, SURE.. I'D LOVE THAT... THANK YOU!

WHAM

STUPID CLONE.

LARRY, I THINK IT'S TIME YOU TALKED TO OUR SON ABOUT THE BIRDS AND THE BEES.
Oh, peese woomun..No be stoopid. Why me do dat?

BECAUSE YOU'RE HIS *FATHER*, LARRY..IT'S YOUR ***JOB***.
OHHKay, fine, if it make you shut you mouf.
BEER

Son?
YEAH, DAD?

Birds is gud. Eat dem if you can. But no eat bees. Dey steeng you face.

THANKS, DAD, BUT I ALREADY KNEW THAT.

3/18

Beeeeeeg waste of time.
BEER

WHERE'D ALL THE CLONES GO?
I GOT RID OF THEM. THOSE LITTLE IDIOTS WERE OUT DOING GOOD DEEDS. THEY ALMOST DESTROYED MY REPUTATION.

BUT I LOVED THOSE GUYS. WHAT'D YOU DO WITH THEM?

3/19

SPECIAL DELIVERY.
OOOOOOH.
Feeder Mice

3/20

ALRIGHT, RAT, LISTEN... THE C.E.O. OF JOE'S ROASTERY IS VISITING OUR CAFE TODAY AND WE NEED TO SET UP A WELCOMING PARTY.
Joe's ROASTERY

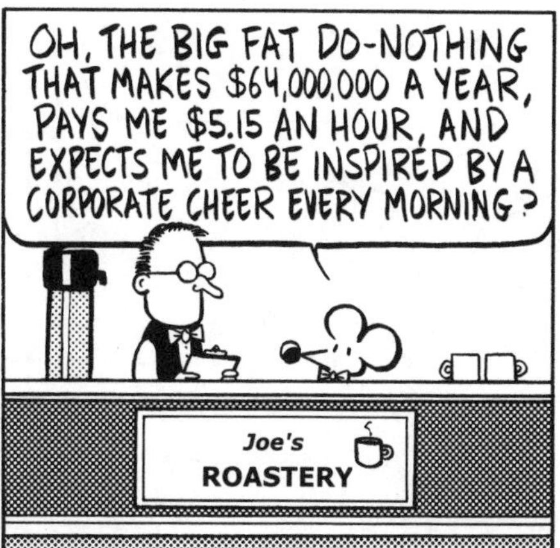
OH, THE BIG FAT DO-NOTHING THAT MAKES $64,000,000 A YEAR, PAYS ME $5.15 AN HOUR, AND EXPECTS ME TO BE INSPIRED BY A CORPORATE CHEER EVERY MORNING?
Joe's ROASTERY

MAYBE YOU SHOULDN'T BE PART OF THE WELCOMING PARTY.
OHH, I'VE GOT HIS WELCOMING PARTY.
Joe's ROASTERY

3/21

JOE'S ROASTERY IS VISITED BY ITS C.E.O.
WELCOME, SIR.. IT'S AN HONOR TO HAVE YOU HERE AND A PLEASURE TO WORK FOR YOUR COMPANY.
THANK YOU... AND HOW IS OUR TEAM OF HAPPY 'JOE'S ROASTERY' EMPLOYEES DOING?
WELCO
ELCOME!

FIGHT THE POWER.
Joe's ROASTERY

CAN I HAVE A WORD WITH YOU?
VIVA LA RATVOLUTION!
Joe's ROASTERY

SIR, GOOD MORNING, SIR... BAD NEWS, SIR... THE JOHNSONS GOT A NEW LEXUS.
3/22
THE REPUBLIC
FLAKES

WHAT'S WRONG WITH THAT?
A LOT, SIR... I THINK THEY'RE TRYING TO MAKE US FEEL POOR AND UNWORTHY.
THE REPUBLIC
FLAKES

MAYBE THEY JUST LIKE THE CAR.
THE REPUBLIC

WISH WE'D SPOKEN SOONER, SIR.
FLAKES

HOLA, SWEETCHEEKS.. I'M HERE FOR WORK AND DON'T GIVE ME ANY FLAK FOR BEING TWO HOURS LATE... I'M NOT IN THE MOOD.
YOU'RE FIRED, RAT.
Joe's ROASTERY

OH, SHOVE IT IN YOUR EAR, GARY.. YOU'VE GOT A POLICY OF CORPORATE DIVERSITY AND I'M YOUR ONLY RAT.

IS THAT SO, SWEETCHEEKS?
3/23

YOU CAN'T HANDLE FEEDER MICE?
Dey punch me in hed.
CAN WE CLEAN THE BATHROOMS AGAIN, MR. GARY? PLEEEEEEASE...
WE LOVE YOU, MR. GARY.
Joe's ROASTERY

HEY, PIG, LOOK... I GOT YOU THE NEW "WAKE UP WITH HAPPY SMILEY GEORGE" ALARM CLOCK.
WOW! "HAPPY SMILEY GEORGE"! THAT'S GREAT! LET ME TRY THE ALARM HERE...
CLICK

RISE AND SHINE, FATTY!! ANOTHER @#%*#@ DAY AWAITS!!
3/24

THE PACKAGING'S A BIT MISLEADING.

I WAS IN THE BOOKSTORE TODAY. I NOTICED THEY HAD TWELVE OF THE LATEST 'GET FUZZY' BOOK, BUT ONLY TEN OF YOUR NEWEST 'PEARLS' BOOK.
GOOD FOR 'FUZZY.'

DOES IT HURT YOU TO KNOW THAT DARBY CONLEY IS TWENTY PERCENT MORE POPULAR THAN YOU?
PLEASE GO AWAY.

AFTER ALL, IF THIS WERE AN ELECTION, THAT WOULD BE CONSIDERED A @#☆#@★@ LANDSLIDE.

I MEAN, LOOK AT THIS, YOU'VE GOT STUPID CROCS ON THE COVER OF YOUR BOOK..WHO WANTS STUPID CROCS? NO ONE! CATS! CATS ARE WHAT THE COUNTRY DEMANDS! GIVE THE PEOPLE WHAT THEY WANT!

I DON'T HAVE A STUPID CAT IN MY COMIC, OKAY?! I DON'T EVEN KNOW HOW TO DRAW ONE!!!
3/25

AND THAT'S WHERE "BICKY," THE QUASI-COPYRIGHT INFRINGING CAT COMES IN.
I HOPE YOU KNOW A GOOD ATTORNEY.
WHY ME? WHY ME? WHY ME?

WHERE YOU OFF TO, PIG?
'SHINY HAPPY NEW BEGINNINGS.'.. IT'S A RANCH OFFERING 'A WARM, FRIENDLY, SUPPORTIVE ENVIRONMENT CLOSE TO NATURE.'
3/26

PIG... THIS IS REHAB... IT'S ONLY FOR PEOPLE WHO DRINK A LOT.

Well this is a silly requirement.
BEER

SHINY HAPPY NEW BEGINNINGS
3/27

To the most bootiful woomun I ever seen.....
SHINY HAPPY NE
BEGINNINGS

....Best. Vacashun. **Ever.**
DETOX

Dear Mother,
Hi. I am on vacation. It is a great resort!
3/28

The only bad thing is that they make you drink beer to get in here. ☹
But I did it and now I'm in! ☺

Oh well... I gotta go. I met a new friend and we're gonna play Frisbee together.

YOU READY, BRITNEY?
SURE AM, PIG.

PIG AND BRITNEY IN REHAB
YOU READY, PIG?
I think so.
THEN LET'S DO IT.
BAH DUM DUM..

..OHH BABY BABY.. HOW
WAS I SUPPOSED TO
KNOOOOOOOW....
3/29

...BETTER?
A LITTLE.

PIG AND BRITNEY AT REHAB
THERE SURE ARE A LOT OF FAMOUS PEOPLE HERE.
YEAH. NO MATTER WHAT YOU DO WRONG NOW, YOU CHECK INTO REHAB. IT'S DAMAGE CONTROL.

WOW. YOU'RE NOT KIDDING. THAT'S THAT MOVIE STAR, *...AND THAT'S THAT RADIO SHOW HOST, *. HEY, AND THERE'S MY MAYOR, *. AND THAT'S MY CONGRESSMAN, *.
3/30
* Deleted at request of my syndicate.

MAYBE IT'D BE QUICKER TO LIST THE PEOPLE WHO AREN'T IN HERE.
WELL, THERE'S *. BUT SHE SHOULD BE.
* Deleted at INSISTENCE of my syndicate.

PIG AND BRITNEY IN REHAB
3/31
OHH, BRITNEY... THE REHAB CENTER FOUND OUT I DON'T HAVE A DRINKING PROBLEM! THEY'RE KICKING ME OUT! I'M GONNA MISS YOU!
I'LL MISS YOU TOO, PIG!

YOU REALLY NEED TO START WEARING UNDERPANTS.

SO, PIGITA... HOW DO YOU LIKE THIS NEW RESTAURANT?
FINE, PIG, BUT I HAVE SOME BAD NEWS.

WHAT IS IT?
I NO LONGER WANT TO SEE YOU.

WHAT? HOW CAN YOU SAY THAT?
BECAUSE YOU'RE LIKE A LITTLE BOY, PIG, AND I WANT A MAN. SOMEONE WHO'S ESTABLISHED. SOMEONE WHO'S CONNECTED. SOMEONE WHO'S RESPECTED.

I'M ESTABLISHED! I'M CONNECTED! I'M RESPECTED!

PACK OF CRAYONS?

THAT DIDN'T HELP.

WHAT ARE YOU DOING, RAT?
I'M PORING OVER PHYSICS BOOKS IN AN ATTEMPT TO UNIFY GENERAL RELATIVITY AND QUANTUM MECHANICS INTO ONE UNIFIED THEORY THAT GOVERNS OUR ENTIRE EXISTENCE.
4/2

WHAT HAVE YOU GOT SO FAR?
THIS.

Beer is good.

I DIDN'T KNOW IT WAS THAT SIMPLE.

I CAN'T FALL ASLEEP, DAD.... CAN YOU TELL ME A BEDTIME STORY?
Sure me can, son.
4/3

Once upon time, dere was girl named Goldilocks.

Bear keel her.

Sweet dreams, my baby boy.
NOT LIKELY, POPS.

EXCUSE ME, PIG, BUT DID YOU EAT MY LAST BAG OF CHEESE POOFS?
OH, YEAH, SORRY.. I REALLY LOVE CHEESE POOFS.
4/4

LISTEN, PIG, YOU KNOW WE'RE FRIENDS.
RIGHT.
AND YOU KNOW I'D GO TO BAT FOR YOU.
RIGHT.

SMACK

THEN YOU SHOULD BE EXPECTING THAT.
...I'VE NEVER LIKED BASEBALL.

WHAT'S THAT STUCK TO YOUR HAND?
A POST-IT TELLING ME TO LOOK AT MY WALLET.

WHAT'S ON YOUR WALLET?
A POST-IT REMINDING ME TO CHECK MY COMPUTER MONITOR.

WHAT'S ON YOUR COMPUTER MONITOR?
A POST-IT TELLING ME NOT TO MISS MY ONE O'CLOCK DOCTOR'S APPOINTMENT.

YOUR APPOINTMENT WAS TWO HOURS AGO.

YOU COULD HAVE REMINDED ME.

LOOK, RAT, IT'S TIMMY THE OWL..HE'S THE NEWEST CHARACTER IN OUR STRIP.
DUDE, OWLS ARE NOCTURNAL..WHILE WE'RE UP WORKING AND TELLING JOKES, HE'LL BE FAST ASLEEP... HE'S USELESS...LET'S GET OUTTA HERE.

TWO DRUNK RABBIS WALK INTO A BAR.

I'M THE KIND OF GUY THAT WOMEN FIND REALLY ATTRACTIVE.
IS THAT SO?

YEAH, BUT THEN I THINK I DO THINGS THAT MAKE ME SEEM LESS ATTRACTIVE.
LIKE WHAT?

I TALK.
THEY'RE SO JUDGMENTAL.

THE UNSUSPECTING ZEBRA APPROACHES THE WATERING HOLE....

HE TAKES A DRINK...HE DOES NOT SEE THE CROCODILE LURKING JUST BENEATH THE SURFACE...

THE CROC STRIKES.

AND THE ZEBRA.... IS NO MORE.

WOOHOOHOOOOOOO!

SO WHEN DO YOU GET YOUR DRAPES BACK FROM THE DRY CLEANERS?
We numba one! We numba one!
NOT SOON ENOUGH.

HEY, RAT... DID YOU BREAK MY COFFEE MUG?
NO... I JUST BUMPED IT WITH MY ELBOW.
SUGARY BLISS

4/9

WHILE THE FORCE OF MY ELBOW DID INDEED MOVE IT FROM ITS POSITION OF REST AND TOWARD THE EDGE OF THE COUNTER, IT WAS GRAVITY THAT TOOK OVER AT THAT POINT AND SUCKED IT TOWARD THE SURFACE OF THE EARTH.

SORRY FOR BLAMING YOU.
NO PROBLEMO.
SUGARY BLISS

RAT WENT GREEK DANCING.
GEE, I LOVE GREEK DANCING, BUT SINCE WHEN DOES RAT WANT TO HOLD HANDS WITH OTHER PEOPLE AND GO AROUND IN CIRCLES?

4/10

OHHH, THAT'S NOT WHY HE GOES.
THEN WHY'S HE GO?

MIND SAVING SOMETHING FOR US TO EAT ON?

IF ONE MORE TALKING HEAD ON FOX, CNN OR MSNBC BEGINS THEIR SENTENCE WITH THE WORD "LOOK," I AM GOING TO DRIVE TO THE STUDIO AND BEAT THEM WITH A FROZEN HAM.

4/11

LOOK, THE SITUATION IS AS FOLLOWS...

I'LL BE BACK.

GRUNT
GRUNT
GRUNT

4/12
GRUNT
GRUNT
GRUNT

LOOKS LIKE WE'VE GOT SUMO SQUIRRELS AGAIN.
BONZAI!
RRRRGGG

WELL, HELLO, L'IL SUMO SQUIRREL... WHAT CAN I DO FOR YOU?
GRUNT

4/13
NO, I DIDN'T KNOW IT WAS TRADITIONAL FOR SUMO WRESTLERS TO THROW SALT BEFORE A MATCH AND THAT YOU HAD RUN OUT OF SALT.
GRUNT

WELL, I DON'T THINK WE HAVE ANY SALT, BUT I CAN CHECK IN THE KITCHEN AND SEE WHAT I CAN FIND.
GRUNT
GRUNT

WHY IS THAT SQUIRREL THROWING MY LEFTOVER RAVIOLI ON THE LAWN?
DO ALL YOUR SQUIRRELS WEAR JOCK STRAPS?

LOOKS LIKE THAT ONE FAT SUMO SQUIRREL IS JUST DOMINATING THE COMPETITION... HE CAN'T EVEN FIND ANYONE FAT ENOUGH TO GIVE HIM A GOOD MATCH...

4/14
UH... LOOKS LIKE HE FOUND SOMEONE.

THIS IS SO HUMILIATING.

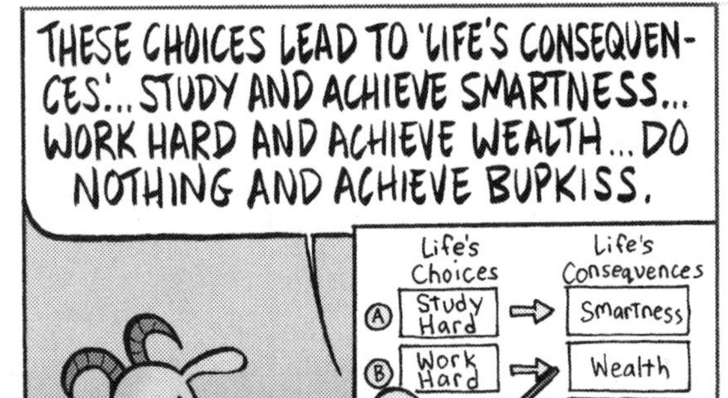

SO, YOU SAY, I'LL PICK ROADS Ⓐ OR Ⓑ, BECAUSE EVEN THOUGH THEY DEMAND A LOT OF WORK, THEY ULTIMATELY LEAD TO BETTER THINGS THAN ROAD Ⓒ, RIGHT? WRONG.

DAD, I MET A GIRL I REALLY LIKE.

Gud for you, son... Gud woomun important... She support you... Help you hunt.

DON'T COUNT ON IT.

DO YOU COME FROM A HUGE FAMILY, SIR?

NO, BUT A COUPLE OF THEM ARE A LITTLE PUDGY.

YOU'RE A COUPLE CANDIES SHORT OF A PIÑATA, SIR.

DAD, I'M GOING ON A DINNER DATE.

Me see you dinner. Where you date?

WE SHOULD TALK, DAD.

DAD...I'M AFRAID YOU DON'T UNDERSTAND... I WANT TO DATE A ZEBRA.
HAHAHA..Dat gud one! Uhh..Me want date..uh.. CHEEKEN LEG!! HAHAAHA...Does you want see movie, pretty cheeken leg??

What? What dat? You alreddy going movies wid mash potato? ...Oh well...Dat okay... Me see what ham sandwich doing.

BAAAHAHAHAWHAW HOOHOOHOOHEEHEE HEESNOOOOOORT
THIS MAY TAKE AWHILE.

WHEN YOU DIE, ARE YOU GONNA BE A BIG FAT IDIOT AND PUT 'CREATOR OF PEARLS BEFORE SWINE' ON YOUR TOMBSTONE?
WHAT'S IDIOTIC ABOUT TAKING CREDIT FOR CREATING A COMIC STRIP?

NOTHING'S WRONG WITH TAKING CREDIT FOR A COMIC STRIP...THE IDIOTIC PART IS TAKING CREDIT FOR THIS COMIC STRIP.

PLEASE GO AWAY.
HEY...SAY YOU DREW 'PEANUTS.' THAT'S GOT CACHET.

WHAT ARE YOU DOING, PIG?
GOAT ASKED ME TO WATCH HIS GOLDFISH WHILE HE'S ON VACATION.

THAT DOESN'T MEAN FOR YOU TO SIT THERE AND GUARD HIM. HE JUST WANTS YOU TO FEED HIM AND STUFF. IT'S NOT AS IF HE'S GONNA STEAL A CADILLAC.

VROOM VROOM VROOOOOOM

WELL YOU DIDN'T MENTION HE LIKED JOYRIDING.
ON THE ROAD! STAY ON THE ROAD!!

I HAVE NO GIRLFRIEND. I AM LONELY. I AM EXPRESSING THAT, SIR.

OKAY...BUT IT GETS A LITTLE ANNOYING WHEN YOU JUST KEEP SAYING 'LONELY' OVER AND OVER.

LISTEN, JOY, I STARTED TO TELL MY MOM ABOUT US, BUT SHE FREAKED OUT. SHE SAID IF SHE EVER HEARS I DATED PREY, SHE'S SHIPPING ME OFF TO PREDATOR SCHOOL.
WHAT? SO WHAT ARE WE SUPPOSED TO DO?
4/23

JUNIOR, I'M HOOOOOOME...

DIDN'T I ASK YOU NOT TO SNACK BEFORE DINNER?
BUH I WUH HUNREE.
I AM NOT PLEASED.

WELL, LARRY, IT LOOKS LIKE JUNIOR'S FINALLY OVER HIS 'VEGETARIAN' PHASE... I CAUGHT HIM SNACKING ON A LITTLE ZEBRA YESTERDAY.
Hahaha.. He cheep off ol' block.

YOU SHOULD GO CONGRATULATE HIM, LARRY... OUR PRAYERS HAVE FINALLY BEEN ANSWERED.. OUR SON IS KILLING THINGS!
You right! Me tell heem!
4/24

He have funny way of killing tings.

WHAT'S THE MATTER WITH YOU, PATTY?
OH, MYRNA, YOU CAN'T TELL ANYONE. IT'S SO HUMILIATING.

I WON'T. I SWEAR. WHAT IS IT?
I CAUGHT JUNIOR DATING A ZEBRA.
YOU WHAT ?!?
SHE'S THE NIECE OF THAT ZEBRA NEXT DOOR... BUT I'VE LOCKED HIM IN HIS ROOM AND TAKEN AWAY HIS CELL PHONE AND COMPUTER, SO AT LEAST THEY'LL HAVE NO WAY TO COMMUNICATE.
4/25

I miss you.
4/26

HOW'S YOUR SON DOING?
GOOD. THAT LITTLE ZEBRA HE WAS DATING IS LEAVING TO GO BACK TO SCHOOL... I GUESS HER SPRING BREAK IS OVER, THANK GOD.
4/27

WONDERFUL. AND HOW'S YOUR SON TAKING IT?
OH, HAHAHA... HE'S FINE. HE KNOWS IT WAS JUST A SILLY CHILDHOOD CRUSH...

World ending.

What dat sound?
I DON'T KNOW... IT SOUNDED LIKE A DOOR BREAKING.
4/28

Danny Donkey stood on the edge of the cliff and pondered the end.

The end of the headaches and the stomach aches.

The end of the bills and the calls.
Bill $
Bill $
Bill $

The end of the half-truths, the lies and the outright frauds.
LIES LIES
LIES LIES
LIES LIES
LIES LIES
LIES!

The end of all that is bad.

And threw his lawyer over the cliff.

THIS IS NOT AN APPROPRIATE CHILDREN'S BOOK.
BUT I WROTE SUCH AN UPLIFTING ENDING.
YAY FOR DANNY! YAY!

WHAT'S THE MATTER WITH YOU, NEIGHBOR BOB?
MY GIRLFRIEND LEFT ME... SHE SAID I'M NOT TALL ENOUGH OR STRONG ENOUGH OR SMART ENOUGH.

HEY, TO HECK WITH HER, BOB.. IT'S WHAT'S IN HERE THAT COUNTS.
AWW, THANK YOU, RAT... I GUESS I DO HAVE A PRETTY DECENT HEART.

HEART?... I THOUGHT THAT'S WHERE YOU KEPT YOUR WALLET.
NEVER MIND.

DOES LIVING NEXT DOOR TO A FRATERNITY OF PREDATORS EVER GET TO YOU?

CHUG! CHUG! CHUG!

SOMETIMES.

HEY, RAT.. SORRY TO BUG YOU ON YOUR CELL, BUT REMEMBER, TODAY'S THE DAY WE HAVE TO CLEAN OUT THE GARAGE.

YEAH, I KNOW... I JUST HAVE TO — WHOA, HANG ON A SEC — I'M GOING THROUGH A TUNNEL... I MIGHT LOSE THE—

CLICK

WHAT DID LIARS DO BEFORE CELL PHONES?

DON'T TELL ME THAT WAS YOUR LAST DOMINO.
IT WAS! IT WAS! I FINALLY WON A GAME! I WON! I WON! I'M THE CHAMP!

SPLOOSH
GATORADE

IT SEEMED APPROPRIATE.

I THINK ONE OF THE BIGGEST PROBLEMS NOWADAYS IS THAT WE HAVE NO SENSE OF COMMUNITY. NOBODY CARES ABOUT ANYBODY ELSE.

WHAT ARE YOU DOING?

WHEN PEOPLE BORE ME, I CLOSE MY EYES AND TRY TO REMEMBER THE ORDER THE SEVEN DWARFS MARCHED IN.

WHY DO I TRY?
DOC... GRUMPY... HAPPY... DOPEY... NO NO NO DOC....

WOW...LOOK AT THIS... THE COMIC STRIP FACTORY RAN OUT OF OUR NORMAL DOT EYES TODAY.... I GUESS YOU AND ME WERE THE LAST TO GET THEM.
WHAT'S EVERYONE ELSE DOING?

WELL, THEY HAVE ONE BIG BOX OF STEREOTYPICAL COMIC EYES STILL LEFT... YOU KNOW, SHOCKED EYES, EVIL EYES...THAT SORT OF THING... AND I GUESS THEY'RE JUST RANDOMLY HANDING THEM OUT.
BUT WHAT DO YOU DO IF YOU GET STUCK WITH EYES THAT DON'T MATCH YOUR PERSONALITY?

GOOD QUESTION, YOU @#☆*@$#.
I'M SCARED. HOLD ME.

Oh woooomuuunn.. Me get you biiiiiiiirtday present!
WHAT IS IT, LARRY?
Zeeb O' Matic

Ees a Zeeb-O'-Matic...It chop, slice and dice ded zeeba..HAHA.. Now we have zeeba milkshake, zeeba smoodie... Even zeeba mahgareeta!
Zeeb O' Matic

Just tink, woomun! Now we have zeeba coming out ears!!
Zeeb O' Matic

YOU DO KNOW, LARRY, THAT YOU STILL HAVE TO GO OUT AND KILL A ZEBRA FIRST, RIGHT?...SEE, IT SAYS, 'ZEBRA NOT INCLUDED'?
Zeeb O' Matic

HAHAHAHA... Oh, peese, woomun.. No treat Larry like idiot...You tink Larry spend all dat money and not know dat? BAAHAHAHA HA HAHAHAHA HOOHOO HEEHEEEE...

5/6

RETURNS
Sigh.
Zeeb O' Matic

WOULD YOU BETRAY A FRIEND FOR PERSONAL GAIN OR PROFIT?

PROFIT.

5/7

SORRY. I THOUGHT IT WAS MULTIPLE CHOICE.

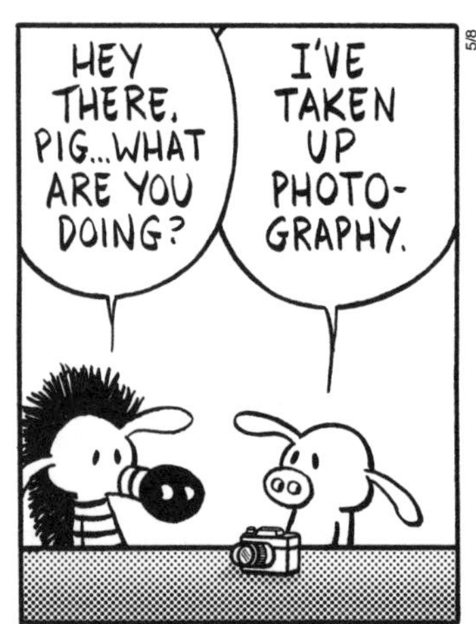
HEY THERE, PIG...WHAT ARE YOU DOING?
I'VE TAKEN UP PHOTOGRAPHY.

5/8

OH, GREAT...SO YOU'RE LEARNING ALL ABOUT FOCAL LENGTH, APERTURE, ISO RATINGS, THAT SORTA STUFF?

I JUST PRESS THE LITTLE DOOHICKEY.

WHAT ARE YOU DOING, RAT?
I'M ENTERING STUFF ON MY BLOG.

5/9

HA! YOU ALWAYS RIP ME FOR KEEPING A BLOG AND HERE YOU ARE DOING THE EXACT SAME THING!
OH, PLEASE.. AT LEAST MINE'S NOT FILLED WITH USELESS DETAILS ABOUT MY DAY-TO-DAY LIFE.

"Today I scratched my rear."
HEY! HEY! THE DRAMA BUILDS!

PIG'S NIGHTSTAND LEAVES HOME

Dearest Pig,
The decision to leave you and your lamp was not easy. All I can say is that I had to get out of your bedroom and finally see what the world had to offer, which is not easy when you have no hands.

Angry Bob was angry.

"I am angry because I am lonely," said Angry Bob. "I must find a woman."

He went to a bar. He sat on a barstool.

He saw a crowd gathered around a man. "What is going on?" Bob asked the woman next to him.

"That's Dangerous Dan," she said, "He's the most dangerous fighter in the U.F.S.." "What is the U.F.S.?" asked Bob.

"The Ultimate Fighting Series," she said, "It's on TV." "I do not like fighting," said Bob.

The woman stared at Bob. "It is refreshing to meet a man who admits physical weakness. I would like to get to know you better."

The woman took Bob's hand and led him to her car outside. They turned on the stereo. They kissed.

And for the first time in his angry 38 years, Bob was happy. Happy kissing. Listening to music. Hearing the rhythmic knock.

On the window. Made by Dan. Who had gone out to his wife's car to see why the headlights were on.

Bob died. Many times.